Merry Christmas Whit —

To one of the
coolest dudes alive...
(even if Susie's company
didn't appreciate it)!

XO,

Alice

THE BOOK OF

Cool

MARIANNE TAYLOR

Running Press
PHILADELPHIA · LONDON

Thank you to my agent, Colleen Mohyde, and editor,
Lisa Clancy, for being so cool as to publish this book.

9 8 7 6 5 4 3 2 1
Digit on the right indicates the number of this printing
Library of Congress Control Number: 2008939353
ISBN 978-0-7624-3549-4

Cover and interior design by Jason Kayser
Typography: Knockout and Whitney

Running Press Book Publishers
2300 Chestnut Street
Philadelphia, PA 19103-4371
Visit us on the web!
www.runningpress.com

Dedication

For Henry, who taught me that real cool doesn't bow to fashion; that what truly cramps style is not that fanny pack or sweater vest, but the deep-seated fear of looking like an idiot. So, here's to fearless Henry and all the dance floor pioneers out there busting new and dangerous moves. You, fanny pack and all, blaze trails where the rest of us idiots fear to tread.

Table of Contents

★ ★ ★

INTRODUCTION

Not long ago, in the hipster Mecca of New York's East Village, a curious character was known to roam the streets. As he walked, he tilted, leaning his shoulders and back into one building after another. He might not have attracted so much attention if it weren't for the excessively loud scraping noise that his leather jacket made as he swiped it along the bricks, cement, and granite that defined the streets and avenues. For some time, the Village scraper remained a mystery to his fellow Village inhabitants. Did he have some physical abnormality, some inner-ear type of thing? Was he drunk? Insane? Before long, it became clear that the Village scraper crossed to the opposite side of the street if the parallel building had a rougher surface: old brick, say, as opposed to a newer polished granite. It was then that the Village scraper became know as Mr. Try Too Hard because the motivation behind his freakish behavior was simply this: he wanted to break-in his too-new leather jacket. Obviously, he was hoping that his leather jacket could represent the years of hard livin' he had yet to tally in. And who among us hasn't laid down hard cash for that bomber jacket, Harley, or hair gel in hopes of discovering our other, cooler self? By getting caught however, Mr. Try Too Hard violated cool's primary unspoken principle: its pursuit can never be transparent.

The quest for cool may be second only to the raw-animal sex drive in generating outlandish human behavior. So what is this elusive phenomenon that Madison Avenue spends three billion dollars a year trying to sell? Is cool learned, inherited, hard-wired into the brains of the chosen few, or available to all with good taste and money? Research has proven that the *quest* for cool drives consumers to spend over $200 billion a year. Yet, is it even possible for cool to be captured, packaged, and sold? Does cool come down to fate—an earned badge of honor for those who've triumphed over grossly dysfunctional childhoods? Or is cool solely genetic, an unshakable confidence hard-wired directly into the human brain? These and other questions are explored in *The Book of Cool.*

Some believe that cool wasn't born until 1957 when Miles Davis released his seminal record compilation *Birth of the Cool.* Some even say it died less than a decade later at the Newport Jazz Festival of 1965—that fateful night Bob Dylan went electric. Others contend that cool, or notions thereof, have been around as long as humans walked upright. *Sprezzatura* was a popular concept in Renaissance Italy. It declared the arduous struggle of creating beauty undignified. The artist's hand had to be invisible, because who really wanted to see the grunt work— the obsessive arranging and rearranging of endless adornments? (Or, for that matter, some poor guy scraping his new leather jacket against a brick wall?)

Cool, at best, should appear effortless, though fashion history proves otherwise. Certain eighteenth-century French hairdos took days to complete, with styles built up over padded frames as high as thirty inches above the scalp. Adornments such as jewelry, flowers, even tiny scenes depicting country farmyards, were meticulously affixed to these outrageous bouffants. Women slept sitting up and rarely shampooed these masterpieces, which were as famous for their lice as for their beauty.[1] Often ladies had difficulty getting through doors and rode slumped over in carriages to protect their precious hair. In ballrooms they continually dodged the candlelit chandeliers to avoid setting their heads aflame. Mr. Try Too Hard might have displayed an obsessive devotion to the pursuit of his cool, but was he really any different than these pompadour devotees?

In its purest form, cool is born without intention. With the right timing and the right envoy, an otherwise mundane fashion accessory can easily become the talk of the town. Oscar Wilde, for example, loved to wear breeches; he found their simplicity and practicality very appealing. In his time, though, breeches were as uncool as the fanny pack is today. But Oscar Wilde's style was a revolt against the excessive, high Victorian fashion of the day—he favored the comfort of velvet breeches and long free hair. And many Brits, it just so happened, were tired of high-end rigid fashion too, making Oscar Wilde with his breeches, natural hair, and loose, flowing jackets the coolest guy in town. To be unapologetically out of style—now that's a real fashion statement. Incidentally, breeches soon made a comeback in the Aesthetic Dress Movement (1850-1900) which was similar in philosophy to the more modern Hippie Movement. The Aesthetes (often vegetarians) objected to the use of feathers and stuffed birds as adornments in Victorian hats. They rejected the ludicrous wigs, bustles, and corsetry, and introduced less constrictive styles—ones that did not cause women medical harm.[2] By refusing to subscribe to the status-quo of the day, the Aesthetes inadvertently created a new, very chic, school of thought.

Trying to define cool is like trying to determine the length of infinity or the color of air. Rather than belabor an abstract definition, this four-section book delves into the many subjects commonly associated with cool. Alternative cultural movements such as jazz, the Beats, and hippie counterculture are explored in the first section which traces cool's history, along with the highly controversial mullet, fanny pack, and manfur coat. The follow-

18th-century French fashion: the height of big hair

Oscar Wilde: King of the Cool Aesthetes

ing science section taps into the biological properties of cool: race, neurology, and the mating game. The third section (business) travels behind the scenes of Madison Avenue to the seedier sides of fashion fads, marketing demographics, coolhunting, and under-the-radar advertising. We end with classifications of the personality types most often attributed to cool, from Jack Bauer's aloof brand of cool, to the beloved cool teacher persona, (aka Mr. S of *School of Rock* fame). What is it exactly that all these personality types share, and how is it possible that so many fail so miserably with misguided imitations? These classifications not only set a few lighthearted benchmarks for cool, but also provide a deeper understanding of our shared human insecurities. After all, few things better illustrate the comedy of the flawed human condition than the relentless quest for cool.

Part I
THE HISTORY
OF COOL

The History of Cool: Introduction

Here we take a closer look at the lifestyles and cultural movements most often associated with cool—outlaws, transcendentalists, jazz, the Beats, hippie counterculture,
rap, and gay acceptance. Why have specific styles (smoking, sunglasses, leather pants)
been linked with cool and, most importantly, are they still cool? How about those fashions on the other side of cool—the ones that the cool-conscious wouldn't be caught
dead in? Do items like the fanny pack really deserve the bad rap they've earned? Is the
mullet really the greatest hair crime of the 20th century? Notions of cool can be inves-
tigated in terms of geographic time and place, because sometimes the origins of a fad
are less about vanity and more about historic necessity, as with the moon-and-star-
shaped skin patches so popular in the 1600s for masking hideous smallpox scars.[1]

Outlaws, Rebels, and Bad-Ass Celebrities

The criminal may have little regard for human life—his own or anyone else's. Take
Jesse James, certainly an outlaw icon of Wild West: for starters, he was a pro-slav-
ery, Confederate guerilla. He robbed trains, stagecoaches, and banks, shooting
approximately fifteen people throughout his bandit career—many of whom were

innocent victims. He may have been a sharp-shooting hottie with piercing blue eyes, but was he cool? Not if he shot your momma he wasn't. Here we must distinguish between the cool, the arrogant, and the armed idiotic bully. Big hairy Olaf (the 'orrible) was the Viking scourge of Norway. Not only did he burn down London Bridge but he also disemboweled and cut out tongues—not exactly a diplomatic guy.[2] Vikings also loved to play "chop the pigtails" off the lowly wench. To play, the wench was propped in front of a board and her pigtails were pinned out flat beside her. Drunk Vikings would then stand at a distance and pitch sharp axes at her head. In his day, believe it or not, Olaf with his battle axe and icky teeth was a real ladies man. All the wenches, supposedly, wanted a big hairy piece of him, because, of course, refusing to date Olaf could prove fatal during the next round of "chop the pigtail."

The wenches of old might have had it a lot worse than the "bitches" of today, yet arm candy is still one way to declare a man's cool. Snoop Doggy Dogg might have looked cool to seventeen-year-olds when he showed up at the MTV music awards with two "bitches" on leashes (their names were Delicious and Cream) but is pimping really cool or the embodiment of bully culture? True bullies reek of desperation, of trying too hard, and this dramatically reduces their cool.

Rebels, on the other hand, answer to a higher calling. Robin Hood, for example, robbed from the rich to give to the poor, not to adorn himself in jewels and gold. True, innocent lives might be lost in the battle, but a rebel's mission is never self-serving. The driving integrity of characters like Che Guevera is hard to match. (And how cool was his fabulous black beret?) On the lighter side, we had the truth-seeking John Lennon with his bagism, bed-ins, and freakish Yoko whom he couldn't care less if everyone detested. Here was a guy who cut his hair for charity and made teashade glasses cool for all time. Of course, being cut down in your prime is always a shoe-in for a legacy that lasts. Guys like Che and John never had to ponder such moral dilemmas as, "Should I appear in that Victoria's Secret ad?" Nothing is sadder than an aging rebel selling out to The Man. It hurts to see a geriatric Bob Dylan leering at a winged, twenty-year-old Victoria's Secret model, or Sting endorsing Jaguars. Watching these cultural icons hawk panties and hot rods is nothing short of blasphemy.

Bad-ass Celebrities

Often the inflated ego of the famously cool gives birth to demons which may be otherwise suppressed. Unlike rebels or outlaws, many celebrities rise to stardom with no more than good looks and maybe a decent singing voice (and sometimes, like Dylan, neither). Certain bad-ass celebrities like Frank Sinatra were known to rip casino phones out of walls, throw women through plate glass windows, and punch the front teeth out of "Jew bastard" hotel managers.[3] Celebrities are rarely motivated by world domination or liberation of the underclass. Mostly, they're after little more than fame and glory, and once acquired, the celebrity may come to the harsh realization that fame feels just as shitty as obscurity did. This often causes the celebrity to become a bitter, foul-mouthed, train wreck of a person, prone to running people over in their cars. Does any of this make them cooler? It might land them segments on insipid news magazines, but will anyone be left rooting for them by the time they get their megalomaniac asses into rehab? Imagine, Butch Cassidy (remember that Paul Newman version) crying like a baby on his fifth trip to Hazeldon. If some tenderhearted therapist asked him to reenact a particularly painful scene involving his mother, old Butchie might have just whipped out a revolver and shot himself dead.

Literally Cool: Pre-Hippie Radical Farms

The American transcendentalists could be an obstinate bunch. Henry David Thoreau went to live in the woods while everyone else in the civilized world "led lives of quiet desperation." The cabin he built on Walden Pond, while groovy, was only 1.5 miles from home. Yes, Thoreau was thrown in the slammer for refusing to pay taxes, his famous act

Outlaw, Rebel, OR Bloodthirsty Bully

	Favorite Weapon	Weakness
Billy the Kid	Winchester rifle	Saloon happy hour
Attila the Hun	Battering ram	Wall of China
Robin Hood	Bow and arrow	Little John in undies
John Lennon	The press	May Pang
Ghengis Khan	Butcher's knife	Fresh marmots
Margaret Sanger	The diaphragm	Infertile men
Che Guevera	Ballistic missiles	Revolutionary chicks

Fashion Accessory	Chosen Enemy	Hottie or Nottie	Outlaw, Rebel or Bloodthirsty Bully
Sugarloaf sombrero hat	Sheriff	Hottie	Outlaw
Chalice of blood	Roman Empire	Nottie	Bloodthirsty bully
Feather cap	Rich Tory scum	Hottie	Rebel
Teashade glasses	U.S. Immigration	Hottie	Rebel
Fur-trimmed beanie	Jin Dynasty	Nottie	Bloodthirsty bully
The mandatory gag	The Pope	Nottie	Rebel
Black beret	CIA	Hottie	Rebel

Henry David Thoreau: raging individualist

Thoreau's Cabin, 1.5 miles from home

of civil disobedience against slavery and the Mexican-American war. Even though he only spent a single night in jail because his rich aunt bailed him out, he was *trying* to make a point.[4] Who couldn't love those stubborn, trust-fund transcendentalists for their raging individualism, renunciation of patriarchy, and experimental utopias? In the middle of the 19th Century, these gurus earned their reputation as the great mammas and pappas of the future hippie movement. They were cool back when all the word meant *not quite cold.*

Ralph Waldo Emerson's essay "The American Scholar" (1837) describes the transcendentalist credo as follows: "We will walk on our own feet; we will work with our own hands; we will speak our own minds." What these idealists valued, above all, were ideas, not things. They were out to celebrate nitty gritty of physical existence, hard labor and all.[5] These principles were put to the test on Brook Farm, the intellectual live/work commune set in the agrarian hills outside of Boston. Its more famous inhabitants included Thoreau, as well as Nathaniel Hawthorne. Yet, communing with nature wasn't so easy with a shovel in one hand and a pickaxe in the other. This brand of rugged idealism was not for the faint of heart. One of many tasks Hawthorne performed was shoveling a giant mountain of manure, which he also referred to as "the Gold Mine."[6] Hawthorne lasted less than a year, but did use the experience as fodder for his future novel *The Blithdale Romance.* The following excerpt describes what happens when a bunch of big brain artists try to live off the land.

"...the clods of earth, which we so constantly belabored and turned over and over, were never etherealized into thought. Our thoughts, on the contrary, were fast becoming cloddish. Our labor symbolized nothing, and left us mentally sluggish in the dusk of the evening. Intellectual activity is incompatible with any large amount of bodily exercise." [7]

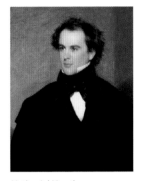

Nathaniel Hawthorne: shoveling manure compromised his intellect

The Brook Farm experiment ended less than six years after it started, not so bad, really, for an oddball collection of neurotic idealists. At the turn of the twentieth century, a similar collective of well-educated British youth frolicked in the Sussex downs. The Charleston Farmhouse was the country retreat for the lascivious Bloomsbury Group, as famous for their affairs with each other as for their art and controversial political views. The most well known members of this group included writers Virginia Woolf and E.M. Forster. Homosexuality, atheism, women's suffrage, macroeconomics, and pacifism were a few of the controversial subjects these Cambridge scholars explored in depth as they played footsie and sipped wine in the aesthetic glory of the Charleston gardens. Unlike the transcendentalists before them, this set was more accepting of their social class and felt no need to labor like feudal serfs. The house and surrounding grounds were saturated in decorative pursuits, everything from murals and painted furniture to mosaic pavements and tile-edged pools. It was the kind of par-

Charleston Farmhouse: artistic eden

adise that starving urban artists still dream about as they toss and turn on their garbage-picked mattresses. Bloomsbury artist Vanessa Bell (Virginia Woolf's sister) described the Charleston scene this way:

> *"The house seems full of young people in very high spirits, laughing a great deal at their own jokes... lying about in the garden which is simply a dithering blaze of flowers and butterflies and apples."*[8]

Oh please, the rest of us might complain. Where is the suffering—the angst and distress that define the artistic condition? Life at Charleston sounded more like a Martha Stewart garden party than a clan of radical bohemians. Yet, despite their seemingly charmed existence, the group did have its fair share of sorrow. Beyond that "dithering blaze of flowers" was many a nervous breakdown, fallen love, and tragic suicide (namely Virginia Woolf in 1941).

Jazz and Cool

What is jazz if not the embodiment of cool? Here's a movement that frowns on commercial success and couldn't care less who *gets* it. In 1957, Miles Davis's epic eleven-sided, jazz compilation *Birth of the Cool* was received with marginal enthusiasm. Some critics called for Miles (famous for his endless solos) to *occasionally* remove the trumpet from his mouth. Yet it was this critical scorn that egged the movement on; to be indigestible was to be artistically righteous. William Sutcliffe, in article titled "Heroes and Villains" (*The London Independent*) puts Miles' relationship with his critics like this: "His idea of a "career" was to try and kick music critics in the teeth with every album he produced." Cool Jazz was an amalgam of East and West Coast bebop styles, which relied heavily on extended abstract improvisation—dissonant riffs that lasted for thirty minutes or more. Who cared what the masses wanted to hum along with on their lousy car radios? Bebop was the antithesis of Big Band or Easy Listening—it actually created anxiety, emotional discord, and possibly even psychological distress. Even Louis Armstrong condemned Bebop as "noisy and unswinging." Yet it is this indifference in terms of popular appeal that has become one of bebop's greatest attributes. Listeners know they are delving into outrageously complex harmonies, which require IQs of 160 and above to truly appreciate. The bebop aficionado can turn ears at any party with a one-sided debate on the pros and cons of modalism. Like members of MENSA, bebop fans pride themselves in being part of a secret club of no more than say, two dozen others.

Was jazz ever equated with cool before 1957? Before Miles came Ragtime, New Orleans Dixie, Big Band Swing, not to mention Afro-Creole, funeral processions, and black spirituals. All jazz, despite its many classifications, has roots in tribal African expressions such as call-and-response and pentatonic scales. Most certainly, jazz is a byproduct of the American black experience. So much so that many in our culture are loathe to trust white jazz musicians such as Kenny G., thus the uncomplimentary phrase, "That's so Kenny G." The following Kenny G. joke best summarizes his style:

"What is the difference between a machine gun and Kenny G?

The machine gun repeats only 10 times per second."

What is it that makes jazz cool, Cool Jazz included? How is it possible that something as fundamentally uncool as brass marching bands could be merged with African culture to bring us jazz? Picture a typical main street parade. The high school band marches by in their synchronized military steps and matching polyester uniforms.

Before

After

Does that poor bastard high-stepping with his tuba and that heinous strap across his chin ever look cool? Or, take your standard orchestra brass section. Let's face it, the classical brass musician has never possessed the same mystique as the string player (oh those ethereal harpists and heartbreaking violinists). The French horn players are often a part of the orchestra for one reason only: this was the big shiny instrument their parents convinced them, and later blackmailed them, to learn as children. The fourth-grade instrumental music program may be no more than a vague memory, yet here they are, forty years later, with a big trombone or tuba still stuck to their faces. It's almost as if jazz were invented to liberate repressed brass and woodwind players from the childhood trauma they suffered in marching bands and orchestras. One famous tuba joke goes like this:

> "A tuba player walks into a bar....
> Hey, it could happen!"

Let's start by taking our marching band tuba player and walking him into a bar. Imagine a team of *Queer-Eye for the Straight Guy*-style makeover artists whom we might call "Cool Eye for the Brass Guy." Replace the chin strap and polyester uniform with just about anything. Give him some stylish glasses, a few bourbons, and plunk our tuba player down on the stage of the smoky Blue Note Jazz Club. Here the tuba player is encouraged to play anything he damn well feels like, for as long as he damn well pleases. No longer must he march in time; in fact "time" along with other musical constructs like melody and harmony, are now pretty much irrelevant. Here in the jazz club our tuba player is celebrated for simply making shit up as he goes along, a far cry from those grueling rehearsals in the sweaty high school gym. No more "Yankee Doodle Dandy" or "The Buckeye Battle Cry"; his songs can be named things like "Effervescence #9"or "Because I Ache for Tuesdays."

Maybe jazz is the sound of regimented Puritan values colliding with all the pain, pride, and heritage of African American culture. How could it *not* make a story worthy of a Ken Burns documentary? Cool, in fact, is one of the jazz styles most often associated with this synthesis of black and white cultures because most of the New York bebop musicians were black and most of the West Coast musicians were white. When they came together, the color-blind style of Cool Jazz emerged.

The Yardbird and The Prince of Darkness

Charlie Parker and Miles Davis were champions of the Cool Jazz movement. Miles (aka The Prince of Darkness), famous for playing with his black silk back to the audience, played despite his adoring fans, not because of them. That jazz critics called bebop anti-music was of little concern to Miles, who subscribed wholeheartedly to the bebop adage, "bad is good." Both Miles Davis and Charlie Parker (roommates, at one time) struggled with heroin addictions. While these two brilliant musicians might summon images of cool more than any other, they both had their fallible moments, particularly when Miles, later in life, was rumored to have undergone a bad hair transplant. In Miles' autobiography, he also accused his ex-wife, actress Cecily Tyson, of trying to pull out one of his hair weaves.[9] And the not-so-suave sax player Charlie Parker, while recording the legendary *Lover Man* sessions, appeared in the lobby of his hotel wearing only his socks. The hotel manager proceeded to lock the drunk musician in his room where he—Oops!—set fire to his mattress with a lit cigarette.[10]

But Charlie Parker (aka The Bird), despite a tendency to sell his saxophone for drug money just moments before a performance, managed to perform brilliantly

Miles Davis: gave up "everything but the trumpet."

Lester's people

regardless, either on a borrowed sax or a plastic one bought at the very last minute. The now cool plastic sax, thanks to Parker, became an instrument of choice for many jazz disciples. This is the stuff legends are made of, a genius musician who made a dime-store sax sound nearly as good as the real thing. Parker died at 34, though the coroner assumed his haggard body was at least twenty years older.[11] His life and music served to inspire many a beat poem to come. Miles Davis, alternately, lived to be an ancient 65, giving up, as he put it, "everything but the trumpet."

The Prez

Nicknamed "The Prez" by Billie Holiday, Lester Young's saxophone career began with touring the vaudeville and carnival circuits with his family's band. He quit when touring in the Jim Crow-era South became more than his ego could bear. He found a place as a highly respected member of the Count Basie Orchestra, and soon became renowned for his smooth and easy playing style. Lester also earned a reputation as a hipster icon by speaking in made-up jargon, so much so that his speech patterns were less like slang and more like his own invented language. He called cops "Bob Crosbys" and a rehearsal a "Molly Trolly." He referred to any musician's fingers as his "people." Unlike many white musicians, when Lester entered the armed forces, he was not assigned to an army band but to the standard army where playing saxophones was not permitted. In Fort McClelland, Alabama, Young was caught with marijuana and court-martialed. The fact that he was married to a white woman most likely exacerbated his case; Young was dishonorably discharged and sentenced to serve in the detention barracks where he composed his legendary "D.B. Blues." Like so many musicians of his time, he died young—at 49—of liver disease. In the taxi to his funeral, Billie Holiday claimed that she would be the next to go. She died four months later, at 44. A fashion icon, Lester was said to have immortalized such looks as high waists, skinny ties, and his trademark pork pie hat. Here was a guy that dressed with the same creative spirit that he played.[12]

Ladies Day and Ella

Talk about hard luck stories. These little girls endured it all, from reform schools, to whorehouses, to abusive drug-dealing husbands. It's no wonder these women could reduce burly men to public sobbing in the smoke-filled Apollo. It's stories like theirs that dare anyone raised in a functional home to hum a single sharp note, much less attempt to sing the blues. Next time you complain about not finding a parking space at Target...think of little teenage Ella Fitzgerald, whose mother died of a heart attack, leaving her stuck with the dead mother's no-good boyfriend until he also dropped dead of a heart attack. She was then thrown into reform school after a short career as a whorehouse lookout and numbers runner for the Mafia. After busting out of reform school, seventeen-year-old Ella finally got her big break at the Apollo Theater's famous Amateur Night.[13] Even fame could not ward off bad relationships, blindness, jailed husbands, even amputated legs (yes, not one but two).

Billie Holiday fared no better. The child of a thirteen-year-old mother and a fifteen year-old father, Billie claimed to have been raped, once at eleven and later again by a neighbor whom the mother had arrested and sent to jail. Poor Billie had done time in both prisons and whorehouses.[14] For all the no-good, violent, pimping men in her life, Ms. Holiday was rumored to have had romantic relationships with the infamous Tallulah Bankhead as well as Orson Wells.

Ella Fitzgerald: reform school runaway

If blues music is about the expression of pain, then few were as qualified as these two women. If their biographies don't make you want to hit Paris Hilton upside the head for cryin' to her mama from her itty-bitty prison cell, then what will? This anger, in fact, may be why the public is so fixated on the grossly entitled. It's fun to hate the filthy rich, to poke fun at their self-inflicted drama, their emotionally stunted charades. Living a charmed life is not synonymous with cool—that would be like believing that the girl who *gets* the pony, actually deserves the pony. No, we marvel at those who overcome adversity. We acknowledge their heroic fortitude, particularly those humble few like Ella and Billie who survived traumatic childhoods without telling the world over and over that they had, in fact, *survived traumatic childhoods*. Eminem droning on and on about his rotten mother can reek of self-pity at best and narcissism at worst. What's cool is when the suffering becomes the art, not art that's all about suffering.

Blues artist J. B. Lenoir insisted, "one couldn't sing the blues unless he had been blued." Others take issue with this stance. Being born black in the segregated south can't possibly be the only ticket into legitimate blues country, can it? And what if your "hood" is an affluent suburb; does this revoke your license to rap? In the following exercise, renowned blues and rap artists are given points based on their ability to garner sympathy. Who graduated from the school of hard knocks and who didn't?

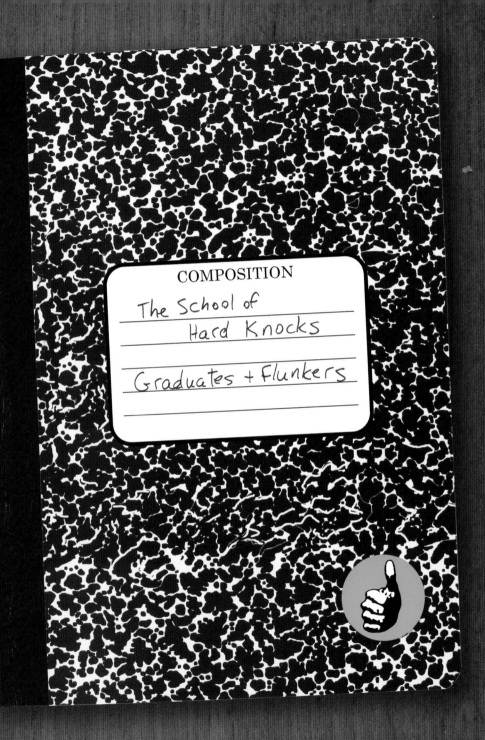

Those who've graduated from the School of Hard Knocks may not always be cool, but they sure tally up big numbers for inner strength and fortitude. Likewise, a life of circumstantial misery is not a prerequisite to cool, yet those who have toiled in the sewers of fate have earned at least a few badges of courage. Whiners, of course are not to be trusted because true compassion is reserved for the modest.

WHITNEY HOUSTON

Origin	- Newark, New Jersey.	+50
Family	- Marginally functional.	-10
Education	- Attended all-girls Mount Saint Dominic Academy.	-50
Sympathetic Factoid(s)	- Abused by husband Bobby Brown.	+100
Irritating Tidbit(s)	- Remained married to Bobby Brown.	-100
	- World-famous shoe-in cousin, Dionne Warwick.	-20
	- World-famous shoe-in godmother, Aretha Franklin.	-20
	- Made movie with Kevin Costner.	-20
	- Saddam Hussein used "I Will Always Love You" in 2002 reelection campaign.	-50
	- *Being Bobby Brown* Reality Show.	-100
	- Fox-fur coat.	-50
	TOTAL:	-270

FLUNKED

KENNY G

Origin	- Ann Arbor, Michigan, affluent neighborhood.	-30
Family	- Relatively functional.	-50
Education	- Graduate, University of Washington, magna cum laude (accounting).	-75
Sympathetic Factoid(s)	- Miles Davis was a Kenny G. fan.	+30
Irritating Tidbit(s)	- *Golfers Digest* awarded him #1 Musician Golfer.	-40
	- Manperm (though 25% of those surveyed believe it's natural).	-50

FLUNKED

TOTAL: **-215**

BLIND WILLIE JOHNSON

Origin	- One-room shack, Brenham Texas.	+40
Family	- Stepmother threw lye at father and just missed blinding little Willie.	+200
Education	- Unlikely any.	+75
Sympathetic Factoid(s)	- At five, made a little guitar out of a cigar box.	+50
	- House burned down.	+75
	- Slept in burned-down house anyway, on wet mattress.	+75
	- Was refused admittance to hospital because of race.	+100
	- Died of syphilis, malaria, and pneumonia.	+75
Irritating Tidbit(s)	- none	0

GRADUATED!

TOTAL: **+690**

JANIS JOPLIN

Origin	- Port Arthur, affluent Texas suburb.	-30
Family	- Father was an engineer for Texaco Oil.	-30
Education	- Attended University of Texas, Lamar University.	-20
Sympathetic Factoid(s)	- Spit on by fellow high school students.	+50
	- Fellow students at the University of Austin voted her "Ugliest Man on Campus."	+75
	- 6 drug ODs between '68 and '69.	+50
Irritating Tidbit(s)	- Owned Porsche (albeit a psychedelic one).	-10

GRADUATED!

TOTAL: +85

ROBERT PLANT

Origin	- "White, clean, and neat" West Midlands, England.	-10
Family	- Father was civil engineer, middle class.	-30
Education	- Accounting school dropout.	-20
Sympathetic Factoid(s)	- Almost died with wife in Greek car crash.	+150
	- Best friend John Bonham choked to death on own vomit.	+50
Irritating Tidbit(s)	- Screamed "I am a Golden God" from L.A. hotel balcony.	-50
	- Banana in pants "If you've got a banana, you've got a banana you know!"	-20

GRADUATED!

TOTAL: +70

BONNIE RAITT

Origin	- Burbank, California.	-20
Family	- Quaker.	-30
Education	- Attended Radcliffe College for Girls.	-30
Sympathetic Factoid(s)	- Difficult divorce.	+5
Irritating Tidbit(s)	- Dad was a big time Broadway star.	-20

FLUNKED

TOTAL: -95

VANILLA ICE

Origin	- Depends who you ask (lied about growing up in Miami ghetto).	
Family	- Relatively functional.	-50
Education	- Dropped out of high school in suburban Carrollton, Texas.	-50
Sympathetic Factoid(s)	- None. (OK, maybe he gets one point for appearing in Madonna's Sex book because it was so sad. OK, he gets one more point for receiving the 1991 Golden Raspberry Award for Worst New Star.)	+5 +2
Irritating Tidbit(s)	- Arrested for wife beating.	-100
	- Stole music from: Queen, David Bowie, Wild Cherry.	-75
	- Comeback #1 as rasta gangsta.	-50
	- Comeback #2 as tattooed metal headbanger.	-50
	- Glitter pantsuit.	-50

FLUNKED

TOTAL: -418

LOUIS ARMSTRONG

Origin	- "Back of Town," New Orleans.	+50
Family	- Born illegitimately to prostitute mother abandoned by father.	+150
Education	- Dropped out of school at 11.	+50
	- Sent to "New Orleans Home for Colored Waifs."	+100
Sympathetic Factoid(s)	- Sold coal in red light district.	+100
	- Sang in streets for money.	+50
Irritating Tidbit(s)	- Adopted mentally retarded toddler.	+250
	- Advertised laxatives: Photographed on toilet "Satch says leave it all behind ya!"	-50
	TOTAL:	+700

GRADUATED!

TUPAC SHAKUR

Origin	- East Harlem, New York.	+30
Family	- Step-dad imprisoned for Brinks robbery.	+50
	- Crackhead mother.	+75
Education	- High school drop-out (though very well read).	+50
Sympathetic Factoid(s)	- Shot five times and robbed.	+100
	- Murdered in drive-by.	+500
Irritating Tidbit(s)	- Shot two cops.	-100
	- Convicted and imprisoned for sexually abusing a woman.	-100
	- Leather corset.	-50
	TOTAL:	+555

GRADUATED!

Hitchin' Outta Squaresville: The Beats and Cool

The beats were to literature what bebop was to jazz, or what abstract expressionism was to painting. These writers, some of bebop's most loyal fans, also believed that spontaneity was the key to artistic genius. The bible of beat ethos, *On the Road* by Jack Kerouac, was written in much the same way that Charlie Parker played his sax—one long, run on, improvised opus. The book was composed, not on pages, but on a scroll of telegraph paper while Kerouac was supposedly grinding on amphetamines. Needless to say, the beats didn't much believe in editing, either in life or on paper. Immediacy and frenzied engagement with the here and now—this was the beat philosophy.

Jack Kerouac created a mythical archetype of cool in *On the Road*'s Dean Moriarty. This character (based on Kerouac's friend and hero, Neal Cassady) was a new breed of cool—not the smooth, composed, understated cool of James Dean or Marlon Brando. This was cool on speed. With Neal Cassady a new ADHD brand of hip was thrown into the mix. Here was a guy who gave impulse control a bad name. He experienced in one day what the average slob might experience in twenty years. His manic lifestyle is perhaps best exemplified in this Kerouac quote from 1957's *On the Road*:

> *"The only people for me are the mad ones, the ones that are mad to live, mad to talk, mad to be saved, desirous of everything at the same time, the ones who never yawn or say a commonplace thing, but burn, burn, burn like fabulous Roman candles exploding like spiders across the stars and in the middle you see the blue center light pop and everybody goes 'Awww!'"*[15]

Neal Cassady's fast living finally caught up with him at 42 when he was found lying comatose along a railroad track. He died later that day. For one charismatic guy, he sure inspired a lot of seminal writing: Kerouac (*On the Road*, among others); Ken Kesey (*The Day Superman Died*); The Grateful Dead (*The Other One, Cowboy Neal*);

Tom Wolfe (*The Electric Kool-Aid Acid Test*); Hunter S. Thompson (*Hell's Angels*); Alan Ginsberg (*Howl*). In Tom Wolfe's account, Neal Cassady drove a bunch of riotous hippies (AKA the Merry Pranksters) across the country in a painted psychedelic school bus. As the infamous Merry Prankster motto goes: "You were either on the bus—or off the bus."

In terms of style, Neal Cassady had more important things to worry about; brushing his teeth, combing his hair, tying his shoes, or zipping his pants were of little concern to him. In *On the Road* Kerouac described Cassady (Moriarty) "As ever he rushed around in his ragged shoes and T-shirt and belly-hanging pants. . . ."[16] This was a guy who lived out of a paper bag; his personal grooming skills were equal to those of a toddler. The self-consciousness required to don a leather bomber jacket, to cuff jeans just so, to slick back hair—these were unknown to him. While other beats might have been snapping their fingers at smoky poetry readings with their berets tipped a little to the left, Neal Cassady was most likely out chasing cars. Ironically, the chic Italian leather company, Hogan, recently released a new clothing line to commemorate the fifty-year anniversary of *On the Road*. It includes a $1,590 leather bomber jacket, a pair of $475 black work boots with taupe snap-down cuffs, and a $1,290 travel bag.

The beats carefree lifestyle was not without criticism, and not only from the staunch 1950s conservatives who saw them as no more than lazy, bellyaching, good-for-nothin' bums. Fellow writer Truman Capote took one look at the 120-foot-long scrolling manuscript of *On the Road* and declared, "That's not writing, that's typing!"[17] Colombia graduate Herbert Gold published an essay in *The Nation* which alleged that Kerouac had "appointed himself prose celebrant to a pack of unleashed zazous."[18] Another Colombia intellectual, Norman Podhoretz, wrote an essay in *The Partisan Review* entitled "The Know-Nothing Bohemians." This was how he described the Kerouac philosophy: "Kill the intellectuals who can talk coherently, kill the people who can sit still for five minutes at a time, kill those

incomprehensible characters who are capable of getting seriously involved with a woman, a job, a cause."[19]

Even Hollywood got on the bandwagon with its
parody of the beats *The Many Loves of Dobie Gillis* which
starred Bob Denver (yes, later to be immortalized again
as Gilligan). Denver played Dobie's bongo-playing,
goatee-sporting sidekick Maynard G. Krebs who dreaded
conformity to the point that the mere mention of the
word "work" had him cowering in fear.

Certainly, some beats may have been hard for
many to tolerate. Imagine sitting at a bar next to a
manic, frothing, unbathed, speed freak who might refer
to you as Daddy-O. In one run-on sentence, he tells you
all about his wacky cross-country adventures while you
buy him drink after drink because he refuses to *ever* get
a job. While the goatees, berets, and horn-rimmed
glasses of the beats might have made them detestable
to many, we can thank them for proposing an alternative
perspective, particularly to the repressed American
teen. By 1959 American youth was aching for the kind
of liberation trumpeted by the beats. As such, the beats
were a precursor to the hippies that followed. And what
could capture the American dream more than images of
hitchhiking across its fruited plains? For all the conservative scorn it drummed up, *On the Road* was an incred-
ibly patriotic love story between a beautiful country and
the youth culture it seduced. Kerouac, in fact, claimed
his book was a valentine to America.

The "J" Man, Ultimate Hippie

Here was a guy who protested for love, peace, forgiveness, and togetherness. Not only was Jesus opposed to war, but also shaving, shoes, capitalist greed, and environmental carnage. These values were resurrected in the 60s and 70s with popular counterculture plays like *Godspell* and *Jesus Christ Superstar*. All this P.R. made Jesus the toast of hippietown. Around this time the Catholic Church itself was reworking its staunch image by introducing such novel concepts as the folk mass wherein congregations were led by longhaired peacenicks with tambourines and acoustic guitars. This confluence of religion and popular culture made the hippie movement more palatable to mainstream culture. As a result, not only Jesus, but also the church itself became temporarily cool.

Ironically, John Lennon, possibly the most widely known peacenik ambassador, got himself into a boatload of trouble by comparing himself to Jesus. Lennon, rightly or wrongly, assumed that the Beatles were more popular than Jesus. Yet even Lennon acknowledged the virtues of Jesus when he claimed, "Jesus was all right, but his disciples were thick and ordinary."[20] Overzealous disciples, in fact, have run more than a few good ideas into the ground. Look what happened to communism, another honorable experiment resurrected by the hippies. The great 60s communes were nods to Karl Marx's egalitarian dream for "common ownership of the means of production."

In their day, hippies might have been loathed by conservatives even more venomously than were the beats. Primarily, this was due to draft evasion, but the counterculture's enthusiasm for psychotropic drugs didn't help. Rasta musicians claimed that ganja helped them experience "sacred geometry," which stirred the critical yet unresolved debate over what sacred geometry was. Unfortunately, many today see hippies as over-committed pseudo activists who spent their lives smoking too much dope and runnin' from The Man. As such, the hippie earned himself a reputation (much like the beatnik) as one who never bathes. Only, rather than smelling like "The Road," the smell of a stoner hippie was often compared to a wet, long-haired dog. Of course, this negative stereotype is commonly denounced by many a righteous hippie. One of the founding fathers, Timothy Leary put it like this in his 1968 book *The Politics of Ecstasy:*

> *"Hippies started the ecology movement. They combated racism. They liberated sexual stereotypes, encouraged change, individual pride, and self-confidence. They questioned robot materialism. In four years they managed to stop the Vietnam War."*[21]

Not bad for a bunch of wet, long-haired dogs.

WHO WOULD JESUS BOMB?

Ten Coolest Countercultural Events from 1965 to 1975

These were the sometimes celebrated and other times more discreet moments when the counterculture shone its brightest—when things got stirred and broken, when there existed an in-your-face moment of triumph, be it small or large. It's courageous acts such as these that define the true hippie spirit.

▶ March 21, 1965, Carnegie Hall, New York: Yoko Ono performs *Cut Piece*. In this radical gem of performance art, the fearless, pre-John-Lennon Yoko invites members of the audience up onto the stage to cut off pieces of her clothing until she kneels, vulnerable and naked, before them. The piece was, of course, vehemently criticized at the time, yet it is now seen as a defining moment of performance-art history for its allusions to violence, war, and victimization. She recently performed the piece again in Paris at age seventy with her 27-year-old son Sean participating.

▶ November 6, 1965, Palo Alto, California: First "Acid Test" held by Ken Kesey and the Merry Pranksters. LSD was not yet illegal in the USA, and the substance was distributed via Kool-Aid. The Grateful Dead provided musical entertainment.

▶ April 3, 1968, Masonic Temple, Memphis, Tennessee: Martin Luther King delivers his final "I've been to the mountain top" speech. King had cancelled a trip to Africa to come to Memphis to support the striking sanitation workers. He would be assassinated the following day and the speech would go down in history as his swan song to the movement he inspired. The strike was settled a week later with wage increases and union recognition for the garbage men.

▶ August 23, 1968, Chicago, Illinois: The launching of and subsequent arrest of Pigasus. At the Democratic National Convention, activists Abbie Hoffman and Jerry Rubin launched their satirical candidate for president—Pigasus, an actual living pig, which was arrested, along with seven other activists, at the Chicago

Civic Center. These high profile arrests later became known as "The Chicago Seven."

▶ September 7, 1968, Atlantic City, New Jersey: Sheep-Crowning Protest at the Miss America Pageant. A sheep was crowned on the boardwalk outside the Convention Center to make the statement that parading women around and judging them based on their physical attributes was treating them like cattle. Bert Parks (pageant host) was also burned in effigy. This brazen event put feminism on the front covers of magazines across the country and brought a surge of new women into the movement.

1968 DNC: Pigasus is nominated for president.

▶ March 20, 1969, Hilton Hotel, Amsterdam Holland: Lennon and Ono's "Bed-in for Peace." John and Yoko decided to use the huge publicity of their marriage to promote an end to the Vietnam War so they spent their week-long honeymoon in room 702, inviting the press each day from 9 a.m. to 9 p.m.

▶ August 18, 1969, Yasgur's Farm, Woodstock, New York: Jimi Hendrix renders an improvised solo of "The Star Spangled Banner." In this legendary version, Hendrix mimics the sound of machine guns, bombs, and screams. Many thought his unorthodox interpretation was unpatriotic, but Jimmy rejected their criticism claiming, "I thought it was beautiful."

1969: John and Yoko bedding-in for peace.

Others defended the performance, asserting that this single three-and-a-half-minute guitar solo said more about the Vietnam War than any other protest or commentary.

▶ May 9, 1970, Washington D.C.: Nixon speaks to protestors at the Lincoln Memorial. In the middle of the night, the troubled president woke his personal driver and requested to be driven to the Lincoln Memorial. There, in a spontaneous appearance with only a few bodyguards on hand, Nixon spoke, heart-to-heart with anti-Vietnam protestors for over an hour.

▶ September 20, 1973, Astrodome, Houston, Texas: "Battle of the Sexes." Bobby Riggs, a self-proclaimed male chauvinist and former world champion, challenged Billie Jean King to a tennis showdown. He entered the stadium in a rickshaw pulled by half-dressed models and King entered in a chair carried by buff, bare-chested men. She, of course, kicked his sorry ass. King was also the first prominent American athlete to come out as gay.

▶ June 27, 1975, L.A., California, courthouse: The divorce of Sonny and Cher is finalized. The duo's show, *The Sonny and Cher Comedy Hour*, was still one of the top-ten-rated TV shows at the time of the split. This very public divorce was emblematic of the disillusionment that many couples felt towards their own marriages. American divorce rates were skyrocketing—living in sin became the smart girl's "engagement." Not only did both Sonny and Cher survive, they both went on to get their *own* shows.

A Brief History of the
Dashiki

What do Mamma Cass, Sammy Davis, Jr., Wilt Chamberlain, Jimi
Hendrix, Peter Fonda, Allen Ginsberg, Dennis Hopper, Abbie Hoffman, James Baldwin, Debra Messing, Mrs. Roper, Marion Berry,
and Divine all have in common? The dashiki! With its roots in
African wedding ceremonies, this colorful flowing robe (sometimes
with matching pants) became an emblem of the black power movement. First produced in the late 60s and sold in a two-room Harlem
clothing store, the dashiki was soon standard garb on *Soul Train*.
What is the difference between a muumuu, a caftan, and a dashiki?
The muumuu is basically a dashiki for white people with its origins
in Hawaii, and a caftan is just the girlie version of dashiki.

Five Words on Disco and Cool

K.C. and the Sunshine Band.

Rap and Cool

Few cultural movements have been as cool-conscious as hip hop. So much so that many rappers use cool or notions thereof as part of their stage personas (Kool Herc, Vanilla Ice, LL Cool J, Ice Cube, Cool Moe Dee, Ice T, Coolio). In the 80s, groups like Run-DMC brought rap music into mainstream commercial production. Before this, rap, with its roots in West Africa, the Caribbean, and American Jazz, had been primarily an underground phenomenon. DJs such as Kool Herc became known for their self-styled dance hall toasts. By the late 70s, hip hop was spreading out of New York and occasionally getting air play. Rappers like Coke La Rock, Melle Mel, and Grandmaster Flash were only a few of the movement's earliest innovators. Like jazz musicians, not all rappers are black, but the ones who aren't have generated legitimate skepticism—as was the case with Vanilla Ice, who claimed to be from inner city Miami when he was really from suburban Texas. As rapper Kanye West put it: "I hate music where white people are trying to sound black. The white music I like is white."[22]

Many rappers have attracted controversy by endorsing crime, overt materialism, gangsta bravado, misogyny, and homophobia. This negative publicity, of course, has proven to be an excellent means of increasing CD sales. Vanilla Ice claimed that his record company encouraged him to lie. It is this hyper-commercial focus that has made rap so vulnerable. Big companies like Sprite and Viacom will stoop to any level to stir up hip hop publicity because nothing sells products better than a gangsta-rap tie-in. According to AmericanBrandstand.com, over 300 products such as Cadillac, Hennessy, and Gucci were mentioned annually in *Billboard's* Top 20 singles. This cozy relationship between marketers and rappers has long been criticized. Many contend that the movement's original authenticity has been fatally compromised. Others claim that for every gangsta rapper out there hawking Nike's to ten-year-olds, there's another with positive messages. Some groups, like Black Eyed Peas, even use their music as a platform to raise awareness on just such issues:

"Negative images is the main criteria
Infecting their young minds faster than bacteria"

—excerpt from Black Eyed Peas' "Where is the Love"

Marketers see rap as the ultimate vehicle to launch fads directly into American malls—as a result, it's not uncommon to see white teens from wealthy suburban neighborhoods sporting shoe tags and wallet chains. Many rappers even tout their own clothing lines such as 50 Cent's G-Unit Clothing and Eminem's Shady Limited. And it works—hip hop is a merchandiser's dream. When Snoop Doggy Dogg wore a Tommy Hilfiger sweatshirt on *Saturday Night Live,* New York City stores sold out of them the following day.[23]

"Who You Callin' Fag?—The Evolution of Gay Acceptance

Gay acceptance—a cultural movement which has pranced from stigmatized obscurity straight into the limelight—didn't happen overnight. For centuries, homosexual men and women have been persecuted. Take Oscar Wilde, sentenced to hard labor for the crime of homosexuality (under the charge "Gross Indecency"). He lived only a short time after his release from prison, a dirt-poor societal exile. It was the Nazis who originated the pink triangle as a badge given to homosexuals in concentration camps, where they were brutalized via castration and medical experiments. Reds, in fact, were considered masculine colors before World War II. Pink, a by-product of red,

David Bowie: the world's most famous bicurious

was chosen to symbolize "likes other men." In Spain, under Franco, gays were also put away in "correctional camps" where they were given electroshock therapy in hopes of curing their homosexual urges.[24] In fact, it's difficult to find a country that hasn't persecuted homosexuals historically, past or present.

In America, the official beginning of the Gay Liberation Movement is often attributed to the Stonewall Riots of 1969. Greenwich Village's Stonewall Inn was one of the few bars that catered to New York's gay population. When police tried to arrest the bar's patrons, resistance quickly turned into mayhem. By the following week, neighborhood residents banded together into activist groups. One year later, New York's first Gay Pride march was held to commemorate the uprising. Before this rebellion, police raids on gay bars were commonplace. From 1969 on, gay rights have experienced a steady uphill climb, particularly in the past ten to fifteen years with such cultural phenomena as *Ellen, Will and Grace,* and *Queer Eye for the Straight Guy.* These pivotal shows put lovable queers front and center. Gay culture came out of the closet with all the pizzazz of a Jack McFarland dance solo. Suddenly, queer shows were everywhere: *Six Feet Under, Queer as Folk, The 'L' word, Boy Meets Boy.* Now, it seems, gay has become the new edgy straight. Afraid of being labeled homophobic, many teens are deeming themselves "bi" until they officially marry someone of the opposite sex—if they *ever* marry someone of the opposite sex. Thus, the term "bicurious." David Bowie may be popular culture's most famous bicurious, declaring in a 1976 *Playboy* interview that bisexuality was the best thing that ever happened to him.[25] He later renounced his bisexual claims and declared himself a "closet heterosexual," ending the confusion in 1992 with his marriage to supermodel Imam.

The success of gay-marriage legislation in such states as Massachusetts and Iowa has legitimized the platform of homosexual rights in America. Homophobia, of course, still exists, but it is no longer cool to call someone else a fag, unless, of course, you are gay yourself. As one popular bumper sticker reads: "Homophobia is So Gay." Many believe Ann Coulter lost any cool she might have had when she referred to former Vice President Al Gore as "a total fag."[26] Then there is *Grey's Anatomy* star Isaiah Washington ("Dr. Burke"), who reportedly called T.R. Night ("George O'Malley") "a faggot" during an argument on the set. This faux pas resulted in a trip to rehab for Washington so he could work out his "behavioral issues."[27] It's fair to say, then, that gay acceptance has certainly "come a long way baby."

Smoking and Cool

From Bogie and Bacall to *The Big Lebowski*, what's unforgettable dialogue without those long, smoke-filled pauses? The following is a quote from a big tobacco executive in the 2005 box-office hit *Thank You for Smoking*:

> *"People, what is going on out there? I look down this table, all I see are white flags. Our numbers are down all across the board. Teen smoking, our bread and butter, is falling like a shit from heaven! We don't sell Tic-Tacs for Christ's sake. We sell cigarettes. And they're cool and available and ADDICTIVE! The job is almost done for us!"*[28]

In 1965, when the verdict was in on smoking and lung cancer, the tobacco industry could no longer rely on slogans such as "More Doctors Smoke Camels than any Other Cigarette." The industry had to focus their advertising dollars into the less scientific arenas of manhood ("Where a Man Belongs"), women's liberation ("You've Come a Long Way Baby"), and into every kind of cool: "Lady be Cool," "Smooth Character," "Cool as a Mountain Stream," and "Wherever Particular People Congregate." This tactic worked, exceedingly well, for a good long time, until the anti-smoking lobby moved in like an angry middle-aged mother and crashed the big illicit party.

In 1948, roughly 60% of the US population considered themselves smokers. By 1970 that number had only dropped to 55%, but currently, it hovers near 22%.[29] Big Tobacco's image, though, is suffering far more than its profits which, thanks to globalization, have quadrupled since 1980. The Marlboro Man, and all the aloof cool that sat with him on his horse, are long gone in America. Before smokers became the social lepers of society, before Joe Cool turned into Joe Chemo, losing both his hair and bad-ass attitude—well, smoking *was* the embodiment of cool. Is it possible that, even today, smoking has retained a modicum of cool, even against the likes of anti-smoking crusaders like Jackie Chan? If so, why? Because smoking says, "I for one, do not fear death," which flies in the face of your poor average neurotic who lies awake nights wondering what kinds of cancer might be coursing through his or her body *right now!* The smoker is beyond such mortal drivel; he laughs in the face of death. Someone who laughs in the face of death couldn't care less about Jackie Chan or any doctor's opinion. The smoker is immune to rational thought. Ironically, however, the smoker is not immune to the very uncool iron lung—as the Marlboro Man can attest.

Patio Fungus

This is how the world of non-smokers refers to the new strain of desperate smoking outcasts. The smokers may be still be laughing in the face if death, but now they have to do it in a designated area. No more lighting up willy-nilly, in fits of rage, despair, or utter boredom. Patio fungus is found in small remorseful clusters out behind office buildings, bars, restaurants—pretty much any public building where smoking is banned. They huddle under tiny overhangs with their disposable Bics, lighting and relighting their wet butts despite the pelting rain, sleet, and even hail. They have no more dignity than angry crack addicts or lepers on dollies—passersby step around them, disgusted that their tax dollars will soon have to pay for their portable oxygen tanks and grotesque little voice boxes. And least cool of all is the patio fungus of any hospital. These drawn, lizard-skinned smokers truly are the walking dead. The whites of their eyes yellow with each deep drag they take. Their skinny little asses might be fully exposed from the backs of their untied hospital gowns but it's obviously too late to give a damn. Clinging to their wheelchairs, walkers and portable IVs, these doomed addicts are proof that, as Miles Davis said, "You're better off snorting coke than smoking cigarettes."

Patio fungus, the hospital strain. How cool are they?

A Tribute to Old Leatherface

Despite the statistics, some smokers do live to beat the odds. These tough-skinned human anomalies deserve kudos for sticking to their smoking guns and not quitting—for smoking in fact, up to three packs a day for periods of fifty years or more. With their pale crusty skin and their gravely, troglodyte voices, these smokers survive(d) to ripe old ages. One theory suggests that the lung tissue in heavy smokers becomes so toxic that it

actually begins to petrify, thus becoming impenetrable to cancer, emphysema, even the common cold. They are not unlike the spiked and venomous stonefish that disguises itself as reef bottom rock. Its green and mottled skin is similar in complexion to the cheeks of many a lifelong smoker. Among our favorites are (were): Lucille Ball, Keith Richards, George Burns, and Jack Palance.

The Skinny on Tats

Tattooing has been around since the dawn of man. The famous, well-preserved mummy Otzi the Iceman (born around 3300 BC) was branded with 57 carbon tattoos.[30] In Japan, tattooing dates back to the 10,000 year-old Paleolithic Era. Captain James Cook first documented the Polynesian custom of "Tattaw" in 1769 during an expedition to the Marquesas Islands, thus introducing the practice to Europe.[31] Historically, these markings have represented everything from concentration-camp identification, spiritual commitment, evidence of courage, proof of social status, criminal gang ranking, military bravado, and pledges of love. Janis Joplin is often credited with bringing tattooing out of the seedy back rooms and into the mainstream. Her tattoos were done by San Francisco's Lyle Tuttle, known to many as "the forefather of modern tattooing." When *Prick Magazine* asked about the popularity of his art form, Tuttle responded:

> *"Women's liberation! One hundred percent women's liberation! That put tattooing back on the map. With women getting a new-found freedom, they could get tattooed if they so desired. It increased and opened the market by 50% of the population—hell of the human race! For three years, I tattooed almost nothing but women."*[32]

Reality shows like *Inked* and *Miami Ink* have brought body art even further into the mainstream. By 2003, 16% of all adults in the United States were tattooed in at least one place on their bodies, and the number for 25-to-29 year olds is significantly higher at 36%. Before this recent surge of popularity, tattoos were found mostly on bikers, rednecks, white supremacists, and military men—often received in drunken stupors. The punch line to many a drunk-joke is waking up naked with a shamrock tattooed on your ass. Currently, tattoos are *so* popular, that the tattooed run the risk of association with the bandwagon effect, meaning simply, "every asshole has one." The development of such recent slang as "tramp-stamp" and "ass antlers" are evidence of this fad's uncertain future.

"Hello, I was wondering if I could fill out a job application."

And of course, there are always those who try too hard. In tattooland, an insecurity complex can have catastrophic results. The excessively tattooed might as well have "unemployable problem child" scribed across their foreheads. This insecurity complex is painfully evident when the excessively tattooed goes out to find a job.

The History of Sunglasses

While regular glasses are often associated with geeks and nerds, sunglasses may be considered the most representative accoutrement of cool. Often an attempt

Sunglasses Timeline

1945: The Orange Shades Miles Davis rumored to have introduced the practice of donning sunglasses at night.

Dark Ages: Chinese judges wore smoke-tinted glasses to mask their facial expressions during court hearings.

1954: Wayfarers Celebrated Wayfarers' fans include James Dean, Audrey Hepburn and Andy Warhol.

1929: First "sun" glasses sold on Atlantic City board-walk.

1936: Aviators Introduced by Ray Ban for issue to US military pilots. Later made popular by feminist hero Gloria Steinem. When asked, years later, why she stopped wearing her aviators, Steinem responded "Oh, I sat on those sometime in the 70s."

1950: Rhinestone Cat Eyes The introduction of plastic frames made such styles and embellishments possible. Favored by stars such as Marilyn Monroe and Tina Louise.

1982: Mirrors Made popular primarily by Southern redneck cops in films like *Eat my Dust.*

1961: The Jackie O's Allegedly the largest sunglasses ever to cover a first lady's face.

1989: Wraparound Bonos U2's lead singer (whose eyes are uncommonly sensitive to light) is rarely seen in public without a pair of these. His sunglassed persona, "The Fly," was created as a comment on pop culture and the paparazzi.

1972: Glitter Glams Elton John helped popularize these clownish oversized shades, which are the only known sunglasses larger than the Jackie O's.

2000: Neo's Frameless bug eyes popularized by Keanu Reeves in *The Matrix.*

1965: Teashades Small, round and tinted to hide cannabis-bloodshot eyes. Their enthusiasts include John Lennon, Janis Joplin, and Ozzy Osbourne.

2004: The Thump Motorcycle racers and poker players wear these due to the audio players built into the frames.

to mask identity, sunglasses detach the wearer from the world around him or her. The message may be "I'm so famous, I'm traveling incognito," or "Stop staring at me," or "I'm too hung-over to care what you think," or "Your flashbulbs are damaging my retinas." Whatever the message, the intention to disengage is clear. Redundant, and even downright dangerous, is the practice of wearing sunglasses at night unless you are Stevie Wonder or Ray Charles. Numerous car accidents have been caused by the wearing of tinted glasses after dark, not to mention musicians tumbling into their orchestra sections—notably Bono, who fell off the stage in Miami, though this mishap involved both indoor sunglasses *and* running backward towards the edge of the stage.[33] So, unless you're blind or possibly a Secret Service officer, this practice should be avoided. It cannot be denied, however, that sunglasses do evoke a certain mystique. Even Pope John Paul II was seduced by Bono's sunglasses when he hosted a debt-relief concert in Italy. The Pope tried them on and was so taken with their panache, he decided to keep them. Many pictures were taken of the pope in shades, but they never made it to the papers. The Vatican, apparently, had concerns about the pontiff's image.[34]

The History of Leather Pants

Unlike sunglasses, leather pants can't be worn by simply anyone. In fact, there is a very short list of those who *can* get away with wearing leather pants. These pants are not subtle; it's even safe to say...leather pants are loaded. Even the charmed and remarkably beautiful must be brave to sport them, as Angelina Jolie could attest when her skin-tight Versace seemingly split up the back on her way to the London premiere of *Beowulf.*[35]

1953: Chaps

Previously worn only by cowboys, leather pants entered the frays of the mainstream around 1953 when chaps were occasionally seen on the likes of Easy-Rider biker types. Unless you too are a hard-core biker dude, choosing these "half pants" as your own fashion statement is a risky proposition, particularly if you're confronted by a *real* hard-core biker dude. Chaps, of course were later adopted in the 70's by the gay BDSM culture. Again, if you're interested in becoming a "houseboy" in the residence of an "old guard master," then chaps might be your pants of choice. If not, you might want to stick with the Levis.

1978: Headbanger Specials

Heavy Metal bands like Judas Priest, Iron Maiden, and Motorhead plunged leather pants deeper into the mainstream. These tight glossy skins packed cucumbers like no other pants a rocker could buy. By 1987, with the advent of MTV's Headbanger's Ball, teenage boys all over America were picking up their prom dates in perms, Trans Am's, and leather pants.

1997: Red Death

As the title of Michael Jackson's '97 release suggests *Blood on the Dance Floor,* is a fitting analogy for the Gloved One's troubled career. His choice of red leather pants? Loaded.

The Short List of Celebrities Who Got Away With Leather Pants

Freddy Mercury, Joan Jett, Chrissy Hynde, Bono (who also, miraculously, got away with rumored hair plugs), and Alice Cooper.

eBay: Please Buy These Pants:

The following is an excerpt from a guy named Brian Sack who was trying to sell his leather pants on eBay. While the pants only sold for $102.50, Mr. Sack's eBay mailbox received over 400,000 comments, primarily thanking him for his bravery and candor.

eBay paraphrased text by Brian Sack:

"*You are bidding on a mistake...I can't explain why these leather pants are in my possession... I bought them under the spell of a girlfriend whom I believed to have taste...She said they looked good...The relationship never materialized... Ultimately the pants were placed in a closet where they have remained, unworn, for nearly a decade...I am not a member of Queen...I do not like motorcycles...I am not Rod Stewart...I am not French...These pants are for men, brave men...PLEASE, buy these pants.*"[36]

...And a Few More Reasons Never to Wear Leather Pants:

They have been deemed "unhygienic" by many because they don't breathe, thus causing the wearer to sweat profusely.

Pat Benatar

Hard to get on, hard to get off. "The lotion and the powder have made a *paste!*" Ross Geller, Friends: "The One with All the Resolutions" episode (1999).

The Village People

Halle Berry won the 2004 Razzie for Worst Actress in *Catwoman*.

Real bikers may beat your face in.

David Hasselhoff

Cucumber required for the ill equipped.

People will laugh at you.

Fads and Their Historic Equivalents

Diamond Jim, turn-of-the-century railroad tycoon, was famous for his huge, train-shaped lapel pins, which cost over ten million dollars each. His philosophy was simple: "Them as has 'em wears 'em." Needless to say, P. Diddy was not the first to sport bling while painting the town. Like great themes in literature, fads have been recycled throughout the centuries. Tweaked a little here, revved up a little there, but timeless all the same.

FAD

HISTORICAL EQUIVALENT

Booty Huggers
Circa 1997

Bustle
Circa 1885

Gangsta Hoodies
Circa 2001

**Medieval
Chaperon Hood**
Circa 1327

FAD	HISTORICAL EQUIVALENT

**Sonny Bono
Fur Vest**
Circa 1968

**Neanderthal
Cover up**
Circa 130,000 BC

Banana Hammock
Circa 1979

**Greek Mini-Loin
Cloth**
Circa 776 BC

Pimpcoat
Circa 1971

**Damask Renaissance
Overgown**
Circa 1485

FAD	HISTORICAL EQUIVALENT

Kiss Manperm
Circa 1978

Male French Periwig
Circa 1798

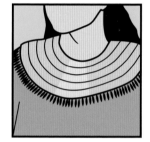

4 Row Bling Chain
Circa 2002

Beaded Egyptian Collar
Circa 525 BC

Buffalo Flops
Circa 1967

Jesus Sandals
Circa 30 AD

FAD	HISTORICAL EQUIVALENT

**Giant Trucker
Belt Buckle**
Circa 1975

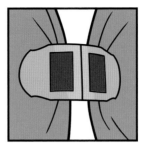

**Germanic Invader
Tunic Clasp**
Circa 300 AD

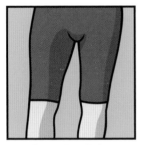

**Spandex Bike
Shorts**
Circa 1984

**Elizabethan
Man-Tard**
Circa 1600

Try-Too-Hard Giveaways

Often the best way to define a thing is to start with what that thing is not. Obsessive self-reflection says insecure like nothing else. The grossly insecure, according to mass-marketing data, are the first to spend oodles of money on products in vain attempts to make themselves cooler. The insecure are likely to try harder than all the rest, thus making their misguided efforts obvious for all to see. Avoid these traps and temptations at all costs.

▶ **Speaking in a fake New York accent:**
This is always a dead-end tactic. Watch Cher in Moonstruck and see if you don't want to duct tape her mouth shut.

▶ **Self-aggrandizing T-shirts:**
e.g., "Quit Reading My T-shirt Asshole"; "Arm Candy for Hire"; "Because you Suck That's Why." These shirts say: "I have no one to love me and stop me from leaving the house in this dumb shirt."

▶ **Ear plugs (the gigantic pierced-hole kind—not the iPod kind) and hair plugs:**
Desperation is never cool.

▶ **Using over-enthusiastic expressions:**
like, "Psyched," "Stoked," or "Pumped," as in "I'm so psyched about tonight's concert." Phrases like this make a person sound as if they haven't left their room in years.

▶ **The manfur coat:**
Unlike the oblivious woman in fur, the manfur evokes an uncomfortable gay/macho paradox. Most gay men, of course, would never wear a garment

that had to be clubbed to death. The furred up macho man doesn't pan out either because, even if he skinned the little foxes himself—he would never wear such a thing in fear of *looking* gay.

▶ **Pre-faded or pre-mutilated clothing:**
(e.g., paint splattered shoes, ripped, slashed or spot-faded clothing). Nothing says idiot better than factory-aged denim buns or whisker fade lines! The next time you feel compelled to buy a pair of pre-slashed jeans—imagine the twelve-year-old Malaysian peasant girl slicing them up with a razor blade.

▶ **The half-open fly:**
This look is as sexy as toilet paper stuck on the bottom of your shoe.

★ ★ ★

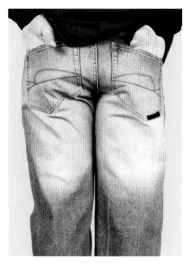

Spot-faded buns

Manfur Coat

Timelessly Uncool?

There is fashion and then there is unfashion. On the other side of those timeless fashions such as KRL (Killer Red Lipstick) or the LBD (Little Black Dress) are the undying trademarks of uncool. Take the fanny pack, for example. How did such an innocent, practical accoutrement become so detestable to the militant fashion-istas? Unlike the previous list of giveaways, the following items do not necessarily reek of desperation or trying too hard. In fact, they are often the opposite, visible proof that one is completely oblivious to fashion—not trying at all. While this self-assurance may be in itself very appealing, it is often not enough to carry an awkward look through the portals of cool. So why is it that fanny packs look stupid no matter what? Two words: *proportional discord*. Often, there is something visually repugnant inherent in the fashion that creates a visceral negative reaction. It is the visual equiv-alent to the musical concept known as *dissonant interval* whereby an off key sours an otherwise harmonious melody. As you examine the following list, remember, however, that all fashion is transient, and any look, no matter how proportionally wrong or downright goddamn weird, has the potential to become cool under the right circumstances.

The Fanny Pack

It's clever, it's practical, and it's the perfect accessory for the guy or gal on the go. What could possibly be wrong with such a no-nonsense alternative to carting around that big ugly wallet? Obviously, adding visual weight to an area better left de-empha-sized is risky, but worse is the problem of "fanny skirts." The fanny pack cinches in the shirt it rides on top of, thus creating a mini skirt-like look below the waistband. Why, you might wonder, doesn't the fanny pack enthusiast simply shimmy the fanny pack lower down, *below* their belly buttons— or wear a tighter, shorter shirt to avoid the "fanny skirt" effect? The reason it is, anyone practical enough to wear a fanny pack does not possess the fashion wherewithal to avoid the fanny skirt. To do so would require a certain attention to proportional detail that the no-nonsense personality simply does not have. Again, this disregard could be interpreted as attractive self-confidence, thus overriding the proportional discord...if only that fanny skirt didn't look so outright idiotic.

The Muffin Top

This visual misfortune occurs when low-rise pants or shorts are worn excessively tight, thus creating a ballooning of the stomach and back above the beltline. Not only does this mess with proportion, it appears to physically hurt. While the muffin top may say to the world, "I'm fat and I don't care" it also begs the question, "Do you have a mirror at home?" No matter how fat, most women's bodies possess a certain degree of visual harmony, particularly in the curve of their torsos.

The Duster

Otherwise known as your mama's Woolworth housecoat. This clownish garment with its blaring, festive patterns and big pockets full of decomposing Kleenex is reminiscent of every mother who ever broke up an adolescent bong party. Similar to nun garb, this oversized cover-up conceals the female body, thus bringing to mind images of the old asexual washerwoman. The duster is what happens to women too fed-up to wear real clothes. Dusters are often worn for days, even months on end; as such they end up covered with cigarette burns, tomato soup stains, and mascara-colored

tears. Unlike the fanny pack on the previous page, this item has the potential of becoming a future fad. Under the right circumstances, the duster could become the next Hush Puppy or granny sweater.

The Segway

Like its precursors, the walker and wheelchair, the Segway provides transportation for the physically challenged. Why else would anyone perfectly capable of walking want to own one? This is the dilemma of the Segway: it is intended for all, yet is irrelevant to anyone with working legs. Aside from obnoxiously tailgating walking pedestrians, the Segway rider suffers the curse of full body exposure. This overexposure draws an inordinate amount of personal attention. You might as well be naked. At least the helmeted biker, even the moped-rider, is *sitting down*. The upright Segway rider is not only fully exposed, but hogs the entire sidewalk. Recently, the city of Chicago outfitted their beat cops with Segways. Aside from crime, these men in blue now have to battle high curbs, fire hydrants, and public ridicule.

Leggings

What child does not know the humiliation of stiff, hyper-insulated snow pants? Even as adults, when winter weather summons the call to leggings, that old shame is resurrected. Again, it's the proportional discord. Leggings make even the thinnest legs appear disproportionately fat— particularly the upper quadrants creating the syndrome know as "drumstick thighs," otherwise known as "the inverted triangle effect." Also, when you walk, leggings create a high-pitched scream as the nylon inseams rub together—a sound proven to beckon attack dogs.

Pointy-Toed Manboots

Maybe it stems from that cowboy suit that so many men, as boys, either had or wanted bad. Maybe it's about guys wanting to be just a little taller, or— just once— to own some fancy shoes like Elvis. Those long, narrow toes look strange enough in a woman's size 7, but in a man's size 12, well, that's just more pointy-toe than anyone should have sticking out of their pant legs. Plus, after some wear, they tend to point up at the tips like elf shoes. Every man seems to have at least one woman in his life that either coerced or condoned his choice of pointy-toed manboots. She was wrong.

Ah, the male hairdo, has there ever been a style conundrum so menacing, so fraught with personal risk? Adding to its complexity is manhair's frequent mid-life migration and/or disappearance. Those radical looks, so edgy in their heyday, have provided endless fodder for the offspring of the cool-haired pioneers. Few activities bring such joy to children as pointing to their father's high-school picture and collapsing in fits of hysteria.

The Persian Rug

AKA: The Assyrian beard, The Black Santa

Height of popularity: 7th Century BC

The lowdown: These face rugs were usually fake and affixed to the face in the style of Santa beards. Like toy dogs, these beards were dropped off at the groomers to be trimmed, curled and perfumed. On special occasions, they were powdered with gold dust.

The Friar Tuck

AKA: The Moe, The Fab-Four Moptop

Height of popularity: 8th Century

The lowdown: This haircut was often viewed as an artifact of poverty because only someone who couldn't afford a real barber would resort to putting a bowl over his head and snipping accordingly. The "tonsured" bowl-cut was big with monks, who also shaved the tops of their heads to symbolize renunciation of all things worldly and fashionable. And what better way to say, "I'm unfashionable" than a shaved hairstyle that mimics male pattern baldness? This "hair crown" was supposedly originated by Saint Peter.

The Dandy-boy Periwig

AKA: Macaroni Head, Fop Bonnet

Height of popularity: 1680

The lowdown: Wigs gained popularity as a compromise to the lice-management strategy of head shaving—this, combined with the metrosexual's lust for "pretty hair too" made wig-makers the most sought-after tradesmen in all of France. Most styles were made of human hair and powdered with ground starch and lavender. These wigs, of course, were a precursor to the Dolly Parton wig craze that took country music by storm in the 1970s as well as the subsequent rash of 80s big-hair metal bands.

Mutton Chops

AKA: Piccadilly Weepers, Burnsides, Old Brillo Cheeks

Height of popularity: 1880

The lowdown: Imagine a guy with a regular beard getting into a fight and someone ripping a fistful of hair from the middle of his face so all that remained were two scraggly, unkempt, hair fangs on either side of his chin. Add a mustache to connect said chops in the middle and the look is dubbed "The Friendly Mutton Chop" or the "Franz Josef" in honor of the famous Austrian Emperor.

The Duck's Ass

AKA: DA, Argentine Ducktail

Height of popularity: 1950s

The lowdown: This trademark of hooligan youth was suppos-edly invented by a Philadelphia barber. Long on top and combed back at either side, the greased hair meets in a ridge that travels down the back of the head. The DA shape is achieved at the nape of the neck where the ridge ends in a point.

The Un-do

AKA: The Grub Daddy, Food Catcher

Height of popularity: 1969

The lowdown: This is a hairdo that protests all other hairdos, a statement against the corruptive forces of grooming. Worn mostly by hippies and Grape-Nuts naturalists, this is the look of the untamed wildman. The Un-do is often accompanied by building a tree house and living "off the land."

The Porn Stash

AKA: The Marcos, Molestash

Height of popularity: From 1970 on.

The lowdown: This includes virtually any standard standalone mustache. The stash-only look became the trademark fash-ion for bachelor swingers at the height of the sexual revolu-tion. Unfortunately, this guy made one too many X-rated movies.

The Peter Frampton Perm

AKA: Waves of Deep Regret

Height of Popularity: 1975

The lowdown: Peter Frampton looked better in his perm than anyone else who dared to ride the killer waves. In fact, he might have been the only one who played this dangerous game and won—as the rubber rods were merciless. Not so lucky were Greg Brady, Michael Bolton, and most of Guns N' Roses.

The Hardy Boy

AKA: Bro-wings, He-Angel

Height of popularity: 1978

The lowdown: Made possible by the blow-dryer's revolutionary "Feathering Attachment." This longish style was the more masculine version of the Farrah Fawcett do. Worn primarily by 70s pretty boys such as brothers David and Shaun Cassidy in shows like *The Partridge Family* and *The Hardy Boys/Nancy Drew Mysteries.*

The NASCAR Mullet

AKA: Ape Drape, Kentucky Waterfall, Camaro Crash Helmet

Height of popularity: 1983

The lowdown: Seen by many as the greatest hair crime of the twentieth century. Short on the top, long on the bottom, this is the cut of choice for NASCAR fans who were (and still are) the first to remind their more sophisticated critics that Bono was once a member of the mullet brotherhood. Mullet cousin, the Rat Tail, is created when the "long on the bottom" hair is gathered into a malnourished ponytail. Occasionally, the Rat Tail is braided and adorned with a single feather.

The 80s Face Curtain

AKA: The Seagull

Height of popularity: 1986

The lowdown: This haircut was immortalized by Mike Score, lead Flock of Seagulls singer who also happened to be a hairdresser. As such, the look required a teasing comb, pomade, and copious hairspray. Its distinctive feature, though, was the 18-inch bang curtain which fell, if you were lucky, over one eye only. Decreased visibility as a result of this haircut has been blamed for the high incidence of "walking into phone pole" injuries from the years 1985 to 1988.

The Vanity Tail

AKA: Poner, chick duster

Height of popularity: 1989

The lowdown: This style, while also requiring long hair, was the philosophical opposite of the hippie Un-do. Stars like Johnny Depp and Fabio made long hair once again safe for men. No more rat's nests though—this time around, the hair was squeaky clean and well-conditioned. In fact, the unleashing of a long silky Vanity Tail in public was a head-turning affair. Free of elastic, the Vanity Tail was dramatically shaken out and tamed behind the ears. Some saw the Vanity Tail as the dawn of the Metrosexual, while others claimed it was nothing more than a cry for help.

The Ho Chi Man

AKA: Beardo

Height of popularity: 1992

The lowdown: Imagine a young Ho Chi Minh crowd-surfing towards the stage of a Sonic Youth concert. This long, thin beard looks more like a frayed rope hanging from the chin. Each time the Ho Chi Man talks, the listener is distracted by the way the strange beard moves along with his chin. In grungier extremes, the Ho Chi Man is gratuitously pierced.

The Skull Stubble

AKA: Flat top, buzz

Height of popularity: 1955, 1998

The lowdown: The buzz cut has long been linked with high levels of testosterone due to its association with the military. Skull Stubblers tend to travel in groups, causing many to cower in fear. Ironically, the crew cut was a 50s emblem of clean-cut American youth. No group tarnished this wholesome reputation more than the white supremacist skinheads who shaved their heads to showcase their racist skull tattoos.

The Gumby

AKA: Eraserhead

Height of Popularity: 1990

The lowdown: Sometimes considered the high-top sneaker of hair, this tall, angular Afro was made popular by the hip-hop comedy duo Kid'N Play. Boxing promoter Don King's enigmatic hairstyle could loosely be considered an unmowed Gumby.

The Art Piece

AKA: Silk carpet

Height of popularity: Timeless

The lowdown: An Art Piece is what you call a toupee when someone famous enough gets away with wearing one. In this case, the balding celebrity is "above the law," and the Art Piece is interpreted more like a hair hat than a dirty little secret. A few of the proud: Willard Scott, Andy Warhol, Elton John.

Geographically Cool

There's no shortage of winners and losers here. History has forever deemed losers according to race, economic class, and the political bias of the times. For example you didn't want to be Irish in New York at the turn of the twentieth century, or Turkish in Greece, or Jewish in Europe, or black south of the Mason Dixon line. Whatever your kind, there were—and are—times and places where you might have to watch your back. Post-war losers must often suffer decades of shame and economic sanctions. Winning empires may ride their glory for centuries until that fateful day when the battering rams show up on the other side of the drawbridge.

Or maybe, their society is swallowed from within by heroic revolutionaries. Despite America's own revolution, England is still cooler than the United States, even if Tony Blair lost most of his cool by singing one too many duets with George W. Bush. France is now cooler than England because Jacques Chirac refused to support Bush's actions in Iraq (which resulted in the regrettable Freedom Fries debacle). And, of course, there's always Paris. Netherlanders are taller, blonder, and more liberal than anyone else—where else can you order a gram of hashish along with your coffee? Some might say the Czech Republic is the coolest country of all because of everything they've been through—like Europe's damaged foster child who came out on top. But even in Prague, the Velvet-Revolution days of dirt-cheap beer and nominal rent are over. According to the German magazine *Der Spiegel*, mega cities like New York, London, and Paris are out. Smaller cities like Amsterdam, Barcelona, Dublin, Copenhagen, Tallinn, and Hamburg are in. Leave it to the starving artists to gentrify the offbeat neighborhoods first. According to *Der Spiegel*, these smaller cities are magnets for the "cultural creatives"—smart, talented young people with money to spend who are attracted to the same.[37] Tolerance and technology are also essential for luring in cultural creatives. In a *New Yorker* article, Adam Gopnick sees young European's view on America like this:

Copenhagen

Tallinn

Dublin

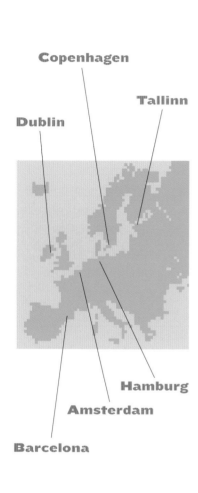

Hamburg

Amsterdam

Barcelona

"The Sarkozy-Gordon Brown-Merkel generation is not unsympathetic to America, but America is not so much the primary issue for them, as it was for Blair and Chirac, in the nineties, when America was powerful beyond words. To a new leadership class, it sometimes seems that America is no longer the human bomb you have to defuse but the nut you walk away from."[38]

It's no wonder Americans suffer inferiority complexes all over Europe. Even if you are not a big, fat, dumb, loud, cheap bastard—you, as an American, have to answer for all the big, fat, dumb, loud, cheap bastard American tourists that came before you. If being cool is exceedingly important to you, consider deleting most of Europe from your travel itinerary. Even Russia could be risky. Also, steer clear of the Middle East. Asia, though, is always a safe bet—both Europeans and Americans are very cool in China, though less so in Japan, Vietnam, and Korea. In Africa and third world countries like India, the first world traveler soon comes to realize how shallow and insignificant his or her fashionable footwear appears in the midst of so many hungry, barefoot fellow human beings.

If you must travel in Europe, be prepared to confront angry mobs, particularly in France. ("No," you must tell them, *"some Americans do call them Freedom Fries, but not me!"*) Insist that no, you do not drive a Hummer, or work for Donald Trump. And, if all this fails, you might want to remind your per-secutors of European colonialism and World War II.

Lastly, if all this seems too risky, by all means, lie.

Canadian Tips for the American Poser

1. **Buy a pair of Roots negative-heel boots.**
2. **Say "about" like you are saying "a-boat."**
3. **At the pub, ask for a "Kokanee."**

Domestic Travel

Angry mobs have been part of the American fabric from the Salem witch trials to Rodney King. When tempers are flaring, nothing is worse than being in the wrong place at the wrong time. The U.S. domestic voyage can also be fraught with peril, particularly in these heated political times. Whether you're a Democrat, Republican, Communist, or member of the Happening Happy Hippie Party, there are things that can be done in red states that would be dangerously uncool in blue states and vice versa. Most often, it is holiday traveling that draws one color into the other's terri-tory. Christmas in the red states can be emotionally charged for the blue-state inter-loper. Such statements as, "Well I don't need your fat-ass presents or your fat-ass house or your fat-ass kids" will often spew from the lips of the traveling progressive who is appalled by the copious square footage of the affluent red-state home and can't help but imagine homeless children living in the heated four-car garage. Someone no sooner says "no politics at the dinner table" than the cloth napkins begin to fly. Likewise, red-staters who venture into the liberals' domain are often crammed into eat-in kitchens and forced to sit on milk crates. The red-staters' simple requests may be met with outrageous responses such as: "No, I don't have more cranberry sauce because I have not spent my entire life whoring myself out for money"; or "Out of toilet paper? Well, I'm sorry but South America is out of trees."

Uncool Blue-State Dinner Graces

Avoid these sentiments, at all costs particularly in Massachusetts, New York, California, Oregon, and Washington.

"Dear Jesus, please let us win the war on terror so everyone can drive Hummers like Uncle Jack."

"Almighty Father, let this meal be a reminder of all that we have: especially the hot tubs, double oven, the saline-treated pool, the HD flatscreen, and ..."

"God, we pray that all the fags, queers, and homos get cured and raise their children outside of our gated community."

"Lord, we thank you for the new Wal-mart so our poor people have their own place to shop."

Things Not to Say or Do in the Winn-Dixie

The military axiom goes like this: know where you are. The first mistake the liberal makes is assuming that everyone who lives south of New Jersey is a gun toting, redneck moron. This attitude alone is guaranteed to incite violence because no one wants to be pigeonholed. The south is full of forward-thinking citizens, even if they don't hang around the food co-op and hound shoppers to sign their petitions. The northerner may travel southward expecting to find characters from the movie *Deliverance* at every turn, but this notion is like traveling to Alaska and expecting everyone to live in igloos. Likewise, the traveling conservative must also take heed while "walking on the wild side" of liberal hotbeds like Seattle and San Francisco. While incapable of violence, the incited liberal has been known to wield a weapon far more dangerous than the fist or sword: the committee. Admit to being "against" hunger and the out-of-towner may find himself surrounded by pencil wielding activists who insist he "sign on the dotted line." Before the innocent conservative knows what hit him, he's vice-chair of the Green Coalition to Eradicate Hunger (GCEH). The out-of-town hippie, though is far more vulnerable to physical as opposed to psychological violence. In the Winn-Dixie, the following actions or phrases have been known to summon the nunchucks.

Forget about tofu—don't even ask.

"Are those fake-rotten teeth or real ones?"

"Do you guys carry gay porn magazines?"

"Exactly how far is it to 95 North?"

Avoid giving the thumbs-up to the big dude in the WWF T-shirt because down south, WWF stands for World Wrestling Federation, not World Wildlife Foundation, you liberal ignoramus.

Bumper Stickers to Avoid in Blue States

Nothing breaks out the pencils and petitions faster than an abhorrent political message emblazoned onto the ass of the interloper's car. Not that anything bad *will really* happen if you don't sign along the dotted line.

HIPPIES SMELL

Cultural norms change with the issues and sensibilities of the times. The suffragettes were condemned by Woodrow Wilson for daring to protest their right to vote during times of war. Yet that didn't stop them. Symbols like peace signs, the Confederate flag, even the American flag, have been sources of both pride and controversy—depending on the prevailing political climate.

Cool, in terms of fashion, is more erratic still. It sneaks up on society with all the consistency of weather. This unpredictability is, of course, part of cool's allure. Would acid rock have come to fruition if not for Jimi Hendrix—and what about the dashiki? If Sammy Davis, Jr. hadn't worn it first, would Mrs. Roper from *Three's Company* be famous for gabardine pant suits instead? To think—the death of the Members-Only jacket could have been prevented if only creepy Luke from *General Hospital* hadn't become their spokesmodel. Without these seminal moments in the history of cool, democracy—as we know it—might no longer exit! OK, maybe not democracy, but it's fair to say that clogs might no longer exist.

Cool

Part 2
THE SCIENCE
OF COOL

The Science of Cool: Introduction

Is cool rooted in the body, brain, or spirit? This section ponders the evolution of modern dance and how this history might be related to signature dance moves such as the moonwalk and the invisible wall. The age old question "why can't white people dance?" will be unanswered in a depth not previously attempted by the unscientific community. Also, the modern-day phenomenon of geeks versus emos will be viewed through the neurological lens of brain-type variation. How, exactly, did geeks earn their badges as ambassadors of uncool? And why is it that everyone, apparently, wants to beat an emo's face in? And finally, mating concepts such as the lekking (mating dance) circle will be studied as their significance is applied to such human arenas as light-up dance floors and Burning Man interpretive dance circles.

Are Black People Cooler than White People?

The following is a quote by writer Donnell Alexander in a 1997 article from *Might Magazine*:

> "See, black cool is cool as we know it. I could name names: Michael Jordan and Chris Rock and Me'shell Ndegeocello and Will Smith and Julie Dash and Method Man and Bell Hooks and Lil'Kim—but cool goes way back, much further than today's superstars. Their antecedents go back past blaxploitation cinema, past Pam Grier, past Ike Turner to Muddy Waters, beyond even the old jazz players and blues singers whose names you'll never know. Cool has a history and cool has a meaning. We all know cool when we see it, and now, more than at any other time in this country's history, when mainstream America looks for cool we look to black culture. Countless new developments can be called great, nifty, even keen. But, cool? That's a black thang, baby."[1]

In *The Jerk*, (1979) Steve Martin played a white boy born into a poor black family. Aside from his freakishly pale skin, what ultimately forces him to leave home is that he can't dance like his soulful relatives. Martin resurrects this stereotype one more time in *Bringing Down the House*, (2003) which includes a dance scene with Queen Latifah that could make any whitey run for the hills. And then we have Elaine, from *Seinfeld*, whose dance floor antics are the hit of the Christmas party. There's even a T-shirt: "Of course I can't dance...I'm white." But is it, could it possibly, be true?

So let's take a look at some of the hottest American dance crazes. Any one of these, of course, seen scientifically, could be deemed a mating dance. Certain moves, no doubt, are direct DNA descendants of the mating rituals of fowl. Take the Swing craze "pecking" whereby the male circles the female while jutting his head back and

WHO DANCES BETTER?

1.	☐ Sarah Palin	OR	☐ Condoleezza Rice
2.	☐ Dick Clark	OR	☐ Don Cornelius
3.	☐ Justin Timberlake	OR	☐ Urkel
4.	☐ Barack Obama	OR	☐ Hillary Clinton
5.	☐ Mick Jagger	OR	☐ Al Sharpton
6.	☐ Mary Kate Olsen	OR	☐ Gary Coleman
7.	☐ Keith Partridge	OR	☐ JJ from *Good Times*
8.	☐ Janet Jackson	OR	☐ Marie Osmond
9.	☐ Tony Blair	OR	☐ Nelson Mandela
0.	☐ Randy Jackson	OR	☐ Simon Cowell

Answer Key: If you picked the first person for two or more odd questions, you are simply wrong and not necessarily an elitist or a racist. If you picked the second person for two or more even questions, you are also wrong, and not necessarily an elitist or a racist. In short, your answers, no matter what the pattern, mean nothing at all.

forth. Other steps, such as the Buzzard Lope, Turkey Trot, Bunny Hug, and Grizzly Bear were obviously pilfered right out of the mating dance playbook. In 1913, the too-suggestive Turkey Trot was even banned from many dance halls. Black or white, cool or uncool, these dances were (and are) simply a kind of species foreplay. And, as with all species, subtle variations occur. In the bird kingdom, the red-capped manakin, the blue-crowned manakin and the white-ruffled manakin, all have slightly different versions of their famous moonwalk mating display. The same might be said for the 1930s Lindy Hop with its origins in black culture, and the Jitterbug which many have called "the white boy's Lindy."[2] Some even contend that "jitterbug" was initially a term to describe white Lindy Hoppers who danced very stiff.

No matter the origin—Harlem, hippie fest, or YouTube—mass appeal is what defines a craze. The following dances may be mocked by some yet loved by many. And undoubtedly, each has initiated its fair share of hootchie-kootchie.

Dance Craze Chart

	Charleston	Black Bottom	Jitterbug	Chicken Dance	Mashed Potato
Initiated	South Carolina, early 1900s	1920s New Orleans	West Coast 1930s	1950s Accordion Polka	1962 hit song
Black appeal	High	High	White boy's "Lindy"	"No f—in' way!"	"Look at that white fool doin' the Mashed Potato!"
White appeal	High	"The What?"	Particularly soldiers	"Love the chicken"	"Second helping please!"
Legendary practitioner	Josephine Baker	Ma Rainey	Betty Grable	Minnie Mouse	Dee Dee Sharp
Most often seen	The Pickwick Club	Apollo Theater	Palomar Ballroom	Holiday Inn weddings	Midwestern church socials
Drawback	Possible loss of morality	Falling over backward	Underpants fly away	You look like a chicken	Angina
Signature move	The rubber leg	Back hop, ass slap	Torso toss	Elbow flap	Hopping in place

Dance Craze Chart (continued)

	The Locomotion	The Robot (aka The Pop & Lock)	The Invisible Wall	Break Dancing	The Hustle
Initiated	1962, and again in 1988	1974 hit "Dancing Machine"	San Francisco, 1969	Bronx, NY	1977, *Saturday Night Fever*
Black appeal	"Why are you following me?"	High	"Mind if I kick down this wall?"	Huge	Low
White appeal	"It can even make you happy when yer feelin' blue!"	"No, I am not having a stroke!"	"It's like...I am the wall"	Ben Stiller, Owen Wilson, Jon Heder, a few of the brave	High
Legendary practitioner	Kyle Minogue v.1.0	Jackson Five	Marcel Marceau	Rock Steady Crew	John Travolta
Most often seen	Drunken retirement parties	Club floor	Hippy dance festivals	Junior-high talent shows	Hyatt Bar Mitzvahs
Drawback	Hands on someone else's sweaty rump	Every other asshole is a robot too	Must drop acid	Cracked skull	Tough on dyslexics
Signature move	Dance train pulls into parking lot	Rigor mortis arm lock	Big-eyed mime face	Windmill head spin	Loop turn

Bump and Grind	The Carlton	Crank Dat	Clogging	The YMCA
1994, R. Kelly hit	1990s, *The Fresh Prince*	2007, Soulja Boy hit	18th century England	1979, Village People hit
High	High	High	Very, very rare	Marginal
High	"What—this is how I dance!"	Higher	Very rare	"It does not mean I'm gay!"
Horny teenage boys	Alfonso Ribeiro	Superman	Queen Elizabeth I	Any guy with a handlebar mustache
School dances	Spring break parties	YouTube	Unitarian church basements	Gay discos/same-sex weddings
Unwanted pregnancy	Must have Tom Jones record	"Crank Dat Homeless Man" (as seen on YouTube)	Must be white lesbian	Exposing underarm stains
Pelvis to pelvis	Spastic finger snap	Heel slap	Big-girl-Shuffle	You call that an "m"?

Whether or not blacks have more rhythm than whites will have to remain a mystery until genetic engineers isolate the "stiff sway" or the "ass shakin'" genomic sequence. Currently, the only evidence we have is history. Give white religion hundreds of years of musical expression and what do its practitioners come up with? The stiff-sway hymnal. No wonder Elvis and Hank Williams crept over to gospel. Jeramiah Wright (Barack Obama's reverend and nemesis) contends that, "African-Americans are right-brained, subject-oriented in their learning style." He also believes that blacks clap differently than white, "Africans have a different meter, and Africans have a different tonality. Europeans have seven tones, Africans have five."[3] Thus the question remains: is the curse of the "stiff sway" a result of nature or nurture? Previous theories suggested that modern man evolved simultaneously in Africa, Asia, and Europe, but new mitochondrial DNA evidence proves that all of modern humanity evolved directly out of Africa before dispersing into neighboring continents. Researchers now believe that all currently living humans share a common African ancestor who lived from 120,000 to 220,000 years ago. So, was there a time, a glorious time before the stiff-sway gene existed? Did it chicken-dance over from Africa to Europe hundreds of thousands of years ago, a genetic anomaly carried in the DNA profile of one lone, unusually rigid cave man? Or, is the "stiff sway" a learned condition—a behavior stemming from centuries of sitting up straight and NOT talking in church? The mystery remains, yet, on that light-up dance floor, with mating displays in full swing, it's the ass shakers, not stiff swayers, who usually get the girl.

The Mimicry Complex: Black and White Cultural Parallels

A mimicry complex is a term used in evolutionary biology to describe all organisms that imitate one another. Some organisms mimic features of completely different species, as is the case with owl butterflies whose wings resemble the face of an owl to deter predators. But often, organisms will mimic others within their own species to gain characteristic advantages. For example, there are several bee and wasp species where the male's coloration mimics the more harmful female. Likewise, if a female is incapable of stinging, her stripes still signal to all predators that she can. In other words, many species try to cop evolutionary freebies off one another, and we humans are no different. For decades, white American culture has emulated black American culture and vice versa. These parallels occur not only in dance, but in all sorts of entertainment. Whatever is deemed cool, or simply a fail-safe hit—that's the thing that gets duplicated, and it doesn't really matter who, black or white, came up with it first. Throughout the late 60s and into the 80s, black pop culture was still relatively separate from white. Post civil rights integration took several decades to permeate the culture and few things illustrate this divide better than the airwaves. In genres such as television and Top 40 music, there often existed two versions of the same (or very similar) ideas. There was the white singing family, The Osmonds, and the black singing family, The Jackson Five. You had *American Bandstand* with its commercials for Clearasil, and *Soul Train* with its commercials for Afro Sheen. This schism still exists today, though television has made *some* strides in mixing things up.

The following parallels are less about measuring cool and more about ethnic spin. A perfectly cool idea with the wrong ethnic spin can evolve into a very big mistake. Or maybe, as in many of the following examples, both versions, black and white, were questionable from the get-go, and thus "selected out" of the culture with quick evolutionary deaths. You decide.

Disco Naughties, Battle of the Bad Girls:

In 1976, Donna Summer delivered her famous seventeen-minute-long-multiple orgasm in the dance-mix version of "Love to Love You Baby." All over the country, couples on light-up dance floors stared at each other in utter embarrassment as Donna went on and on and on. The intimate vocalizations were supposedly recorded in dimmed lights with Summer, face down, humping the recording studio floor. When asked about the validity of these recording studio rumors, Summer clarified, "No, I was on my back."[4]

In 1978's *Grease,* Olivia Newton-John's character went from the virginal girl-next-door to John Travolta's raunchy fairground bitch. In black spandex pants, she stamped out her cigarette and, in stiletto heels, kicked the groveling Travolta down into the dust. In the funhouse, Olivia delivers her naughtiest lyric to date, "feel your way," while caressing her own spandex, at which point Travolta lets out a James Brown scream and again falls to the ground. Olivia outdid herself again a few years later as a sex-crazed physical trainer. In this music video "Physical," a leg-warmer-ed Olivia humps an obese, half-naked man on the massage table while singing, "I wanna get animal...let's get into animal."

Do Double Olsens Equal One Emanuel Lewis?

The 80s were famous for bad sitcoms. Producers had this formula which involved dis-gracefully cute kids with freakish adult mannerisms like Gary Coleman and Ricky Schroeder. But ABC went over the top with *Webster* and *Full House*. In Webster, Emanuel Lewis plays a poor orphan child whose parents die in a car accident (yes, really) and is adopted by an affluent white couple. Lewis, a teenage midget, plays a character who is just slightly older than a toddler. In one episode, Webster is found "in his birthday suit" with a five-year-old girlfriend—which might not have been so creepy if he wasn't actually sixteen when the episode was shot.

In *Full House,* we have a widowed dad struggling to raise his family in Whackyville, USA. This show honey-sweetened such issues as running away, child abuse, and eating disorders. Little Michelle (played by both Olsen twins) was famous for such grating phrases as "You got it, dude!" Michelle's uber-maturity and relentless sense of entitlement helped viewers love and appreciate their own children as never before.

Archie or George: Pick Your Racist Nutcase

704 Hauser Street in Queens was where Norman Lear cast his 1971 groundbreaking sitcom, *All in the Family*, with Archie Bunker as a white, working class bigot. He was the first to use such epithets as "dago," "wop," "spic,"" fag," "chink," and "spade" on television. Recorded in front of a live studio audience, the producers took pride in the show's authentic, rather than canned, laughter. Archie's prejudice was not limited to race, he was equally appalled by liberals, gays, and feminists.

The Jeffersons, launched in 1975, lived in a "de-luxe apartment in the sky-ie-ie." George Jefferson made his first non-appearance in *All in the Family* when he refused to enter the racist home of Archie Bunker. But George was guilty of similar sentiments himself, always referring to the mixed race couple that lived in the apartment next door as "zebras." Bentley, his whiter-than-white British neighbor, regularly had Jefferson's door slammed in his face mid-sentence. George Jefferson was also the first black man to use the term "honky" on national television.

Dance Like an Egyptian or Moonwalk?

In 1983, Michael Jackson immortalized the moonwalk on the show Motown 25, but the mechanics of the dance move were first presented by the manic French mimester Marcel Marceau. The first actual moonwalk on television (aside from Neil Armstrong in 1969) was done by street dance pioneer Jeffrey Daniel on Britain's *Top of the Pops*. This seamless backslide appears to defy the laws of physics, particularly when white people do it. A few of the brave are: Scott Evil, Drew Barrymore, and Michael J. Fox.

Supposedly, the Bangles' 1986 number-one hit "Walk Like an Egyptian" was added to their *Different Light* album as a joke. As a result, white kids, all over the country were prancing around with L-shaped arms for years. After the 9/11 attacks, the song was deemed inappropriate by corporate radio giant Clear Channel because of its "Arab connection."[5]

Jennifer or Kevin: who would you rather dump water on?

In 1983's *Flashdance*, the half-black Jennifer Beals was an exotic dancer by night, a welder by day, and a maniac on the floor. In a dramatically silhouetted warehouse montage, Jennifer attempts to dance off her anger. Her little feet pound the floor in their tattered leg warmers as she launches herself into an impossibly long, multiple-shot, aerial leap. It should be noted that the "Maniac" video featured copious footage of Jennifer's high-cut leotard-ed ass and could therefore be seen as a precursor to the booty videos to come.

"He's a big city kid in a small town...they said he'd never win...he knew he had to..."
reads the promotional tag for *Footloose*. In this 1984 classic, Kevin Bacon fights The
Man (in this case an evil rock-a-phobic high-school principal and preacher) finally
making dance, rock, and Sony Walkmans safe for the youth of small-town America.
In the movie's trademark scene, misunderstood Kevin *also* attempts to *dance off* his
anger on a Volkswagen, in a warehouse, and miraculously, on parallel bars which just
happen to be standing around. (Could he possibly be dancing through a parallel-bar
storage facility?) The montage is rife with splayed-open jazz hands, feigned sobbing,
and—you guessed it—an impossibly long, multiple shot, aerial leap.

Travis or Bobby "Tune in, I dare you"

Talk about watching a train wreck. MTV's reality show *Meet the Barkers* premiered in
2005. The series followed the dysfunctional melodrama of former Blink-182 drummer Travis Barker and his on-again-off-again, ex-miss-USA wife, Shanna Moakler.
Travis is known for the Cadillac emblem with surrounding mud-flap girls tattooed
onto his chest. He also has, tattooed onto his neck, the very deep if not somewhat
confusing quote: "Chaos often Breeds Life, When Order Breeds Habit."

Bobby Brown has been plagued with allegations of Whitney abuse, drunk driving, and failure to make child-support payments. Bravo's *Being Bobby Brown*, also premiering in 2005, took viewers inside the Brown/Houston household. "I think it's our relationship with God that we have that have made us the power couple we are," Brown has said of his marriage to Houston. In one episode, Bobby speaks of the time he had to dig a "dookie bubble" out of Whitney's constipated butt.[6] The greatest love of all?

Where White or Black Men Fear to Tread

White people "acting" black is currently associated with terms like "wangster," yet many white artists have aspired to more positive aspects of black culture. Black people "acting" white, accordingly, has garnered its criticism with terms like "Oreo" and "Carlton," the *Fresh Prince* character who realized his dream of attending Princeton. The following are examples of artists who have transcended cultural barriers, black and white. Some did it subtly, with dignity and finesse, while others did it with all the grace of a foghorn. Love them or hate them, these entertainers, either inadvertently or very intentionally, rammed head-on into the politics of race.

Tony Bennett

The first time young Antonio Dominick Benedetto sang in a nightclub was with black trombonist Tyree Glenn. He was the only white face on the stage when he opened up for Pearl Bailey a few years later in Greenwich Village. He was also the first white singer to record with Count Basie. Basie thought Tony Bennett was one of the few white singers out there who really knew how to swing. When Tony asked him about possibly changing his act, Basie replied, "Why change an apple?"[7] In 1945, while stationed in Germany, Bennett ran into a friend from high school who happened to be black. Together they went to a restaurant, apparently shocking their fellow soldiers and superior officers. Bennett was demoted to menial duties as a result of the incident. Years later, when his good friend Harry Belafonte asked him to march for civil rights, Tony didn't have to think twice. In 1965, he took part in the famous march from Selma to Montgomery. He also refused to perform in South Africa while it was under apartheid rule. Tony Bennett's authentic cool has stood the test of time. Not only is he a master crooner, but he's also an accomplished painter. How many shriveling, grey-haired, lounge singers could land an *MTV Unplugged* special, a duet with Christine Aguilera on *Saturday Night Live*, and a gig on *American Idol?*

Sammy Davis, Junior

"Being a star has made it possible for me to get insulted in places where the average Negro could never hope to go and get insulted."[8] With his dangling cigarette and hipster slang, Sammy Davis, Junior, was rarely accused of acting white; what he was most often accused of was trying to become white. In 1954, he rattled the race barriers by becoming the first (and possibly only) African American entertainer to convert to Judaism. In the 50s he had a renowned affair with actress Kim Novak which threatened to end both their careers. Finally, Harry Cohn, the president of Columbia Pictures, commanded the lovers to split.[9] In 1960 Davis married the very white Swedish actress May Brit—this at a time when interracial marriage was banned in over thirty states. "May was young and beautiful but she was caught in the prison of my skin," he said.[10] He baffled the black community again in 1972 when he hugged tricky Dick Nixon

Sammy Davis, Jr.: hipster legend

at the 1972 Republican National Convention. But his propensity to rile up race relations might be best illustrated with his guest appearance on Norman Lear's *All in the Family*. Sammy, playing himself, showed up at 704 Hauser Street to retrieve the wallet he accidentally left in Archie's cab. When asked to pose next to Archie for a photo, Sammy planted a big black kiss right on his face.

Whoopi Goldberg

"I am an artist; art has no color or sex."[11] Goldberg has referred to herself as a "Jewish-American Princess." In 1993, Whoopi and her then rumored boyfriend, Ted Danson, were the subject of much debate when Ted dressed up in blackface to roast Whoopi at a Friar's Club affair. Danson's routine was peppered with raunchy sex jokes and, yes, even the "n" word. Montel Williams, among others, walked out in protest. Whoopi defended Danson, "It takes a whole lot of courage to come out in blackface in front of 3,000 people," she told her confused audience, "I don't care if you don't like it. I do."[12] *Spook Show,* the one-woman show that launched her career included a monologue about a little black girl that wanted long blond hair so she could be in the movies. Another monologue focused on a 13-year-old girl who used a coat hanger to give herself an abortion.[13] The subject of abortion recently caused Whoopi controversy on *The View* when Elizabeth Hasselbeck, the blond co-host that liberals love to hate, commented that proposed financial stipends might prevent many women with unwanted pregnancies from having abortions. Fellow co-host Goldberg asked Hasselbeck if she had ever been in the position of needing an abortion. "Most women," Goldberg told Hasselbeck, "do not have them with some sort of party going on."[14] Like her or not, Whoopi speaks her mind and has never let the critics keep her down. You've got to be one brave black woman to star is such films as *Sister Act, Jumpin' Jack Flash* and *Star Trek: The Next Generation.*

Justin Timberlake

Here's the guy that supposedly lost his "ghetto pass" when he ripped off Janet Jackson's boob cup at the 2004 Super Bowl. But how did he get that "ghetto pass" in the first place, and if he lost it, where did it go? In 2003, the solo Timberlake won the Best R&B Act at the Music of Black Origin Awards; *Soul Train* even nominated him for 2003's Best Male R&B Album and Single. How could a kid who got his start as a Mouseketeer—whose falsetto is possibly higher than Frankie Valli and Leo Sayer put together—how could he possibly land collaborations with such high rollers in black entertainment as The Black Eyed Peas, Nelly, Snoop Dogg, and 50 Cent? Is it because he's that good? Love him or hate him, this 'NSync graduate can carry a show. Pete Wentz, bassist for Fall Out Boy, summed up Timberlake's unlikely appeal: "You can go to hipster clubs, and they like it (Timberlake). I think at first they liked him ironically, but now they just like him."[15] Punk promoter, Tony Croasdale has also alleged that Justin has "major fans in the anarchist punk community."[16] Whether or not Timberlake lost his ghetto pass by exposing Janet's boob, or apologizing for it later at the Grammy Awards, is still a subject of intense national debate. Despite the Nipplegate affair, Timberlake still enjoys almost as much black radio airplay as white rapper Eminem. Unlike Eminem however, Timberlake has never been accused of raping his own mother (lyrically, of course), homophobia, or glorifying violence.

Brain Science: The Geeks Versus the Emos

While the chicken-dance sequence may still take DNA decoders another hundred years to isolate, scientists have made tremendous strides in the study of brain science. Artists, for example, tend to be right-brain dominant. They are intuitive, spontaneous, and aesthetically driven. Since the right side of the brain controls the left side of the body, artists are three times more likely to be left-handed. Some recent stud-

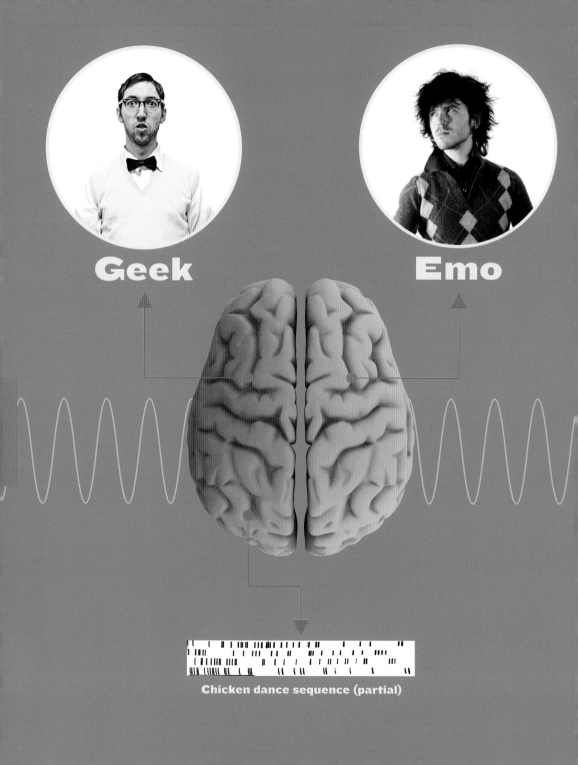

Geek

Emo

Chicken dance sequence (partial)

ies suggest that the brains of highly creative people even have increased serotonin transporters and dopamine receptors.[17] Theoretically, this means they are more prone to depression or mania. Left-brained people, on the other hand, tend to be more linear, logical, and accuracy driven. They tend to rotate their car tires, and painstakingly balance their checkbooks, whereas right-brain artistic types may not even be able to *find* their checkbooks. According to brain science, much of our personality comes down to these variations in wiring. What does any of this have to do with cool? Two words: social cues.

If geeks are social disasters, then shouldn't the opposite end of the spectrum breed highly adept social hipsters? Unfortunately, it's not that easy. It's true, right-brained people may be notoriously bad at algebra and programming their VCRs, but they're highly attuned to social cues. The geeks may kick the right-brains' asses at Scrabble, but they have been known to hover uneasily around the party punchbowl. Geek, dork, nerd, dweeb, pick your label; none are the least bit flattering. And most of these negative stereotypes were earned by deficits in the social cue department. One geek joke goes like this:

"A geek walks into a party . . . and that's it . . . he just stands there."

For the left-brained nerd, many neurological functions associated with right-brain activity, are painfully challenging. These limitations are often described as Mind Blindness: lack of a theory of mind—the inability to recognize the thoughts and feelings of others.[18] Many exceedingly intelligent geeks claim to have great difficulty reading facial expressions, understanding certain types of humor, and feeling empathy. Subtleties like sarcasm and metaphor are lost to many a brilliant mathematician. Also common: a propensity for memorization and repetition associated with the dreaded social condition know as CPD: Compulsive Pun Disorder (also a medically proven sex repellent).

Meanwhile on the other side of the brain...the more artistic right-brained party-goer is reading social cues all over the room. But does this heightened awareness translate into highly adept social behavior (i.e., cool)? No, because the sensitive artistic types often read the faces of their fellow party goers and conclude: "Everyone is whispering about me!" While this over-sensitivity often breeds paranoia, it rarely results in socially awkward behavior such as a ten-minute episode of compulsive punning. Even if everyone at the party really is whispering about the geek it hardly matters, because the geek may be oblivious to their injured expressions as he offers up another round of zinger puns. The geek, therefore, is rarely guilty of the cardinal sin of uncool: trying too hard. Not that linear thinkers don't take the occasional stab at cool, they do. Yet it's the appearance-obsessed artistic types that are most often guilty of trying-too-hard.

The Rise of the Geek

No doubt about it, geek culture has experienced a spurt of exponential growth. Gone are the days when Trekkies with poor social skills toiled in utter isolation. Geekdom has been glorified as never before—the day of the geek has come, thanks to the IT revolution. The following are just a few of the recent television shows that celebrate geek culture: *Freaks and Geeks* (2000), *Beat the Geeks* (2001), *Beauty and the Geek* (2005), *The Office* (2005), *The IT Crowd* (2006), *Planet Nerd* (2007), and *The Big Bang Theory* (2007). Iconic geek characters like Tina Fey's Liz Lemon or America Ferrara's Betty Suarez have thrown awkward smart girls into the limelight. Even *Star Trek* is getting a cool make-over with uber-atmosphere creator JJ Abrams at the helm. San Diego's latest Comic-Con convention was forced to close its traditional open registration to accommodate crowding. As a result, scalped tickets were selling for hundreds on E-Bay. Recently, over 35,000 geeks from all over the planet gathered at the Los Angeles Convention Center for the largest *Star Wars* celebration ever held. This increasingly popular event has been referred to as the epicenter of the nerd population explosion. A 600% increase in the number of female attendees in Princess Leia costumes is seen by some as a key indicator that geek fertility rates are indeed soaring. There is even a geek music festival called Nerdapalooza.

The World Wide Web made it possible for geeks (who previously remained culturally isolated as adults) to find each other on hobbyist chat boards, newsrooms, and other online communities. The IT revolution also brought geeks *physically* together, out of their dark basements and into the fertile cube farms of such companies as IBM, Intel, and Sun Microsystems. There, geeks bonded and copulated as never before. Bryna Siegel, head of the PDD (Pervasive Development Disorders) clinic at UCSF has commented on the meteoric growth of what had previously been a very socially isolated demographic:

> *"In another historical time, these men would have become monks, developing new ink for early printing presses. Suddenly they're making $150,000 a year with stock options. They're reproducing at a much higher rate."*[19]

Pervasive Development Disorders refer to the spectrum that neuroscientists use to measure more severe social disorders such as autism and Aspergers syndrome. While one end of the spectrum consists of debilitating developmental delays, the other includes high-functioning, hyper-intelligent, "eccentric" personality profiles. Many who work in the tech superhold of Silicon Valley proudly diagnose themselves with ODD—the new cutting edge acronym for, well...odd. In *Wired Magazine*, Steve Silberman wrote:

> *"In the geek warrens of engineering and R&D, social graces are beside the point. You can be as off-the-wall as you want to be, but if your code is bulletproof, no one's going to point out that you've been wearing the same shirt for two weeks."*[20]

So what if the left-brained nerds tell one too many puns at the office Christmas party? So what if they might to talk a little too loud, be somewhat uncoordinated, and cinch their belts way up to their ribcages? Remember, the techies out there are cashing in big while the starving poet-philosophers are still eating Goya beans straight out of the can. Why then is "uncool" so deeply embedded in the definition of geeks and nerds? Sure, it might be cool to be uncool—even to be proud to be uncool. But it all comes down to entering that party, and that has everything to do with social cues. For example, it would be highly unlikely for a self-proclaimed geek to *read* a crowd, to intuitively know that the subtle gesture of a half-smile will most intrigue this particular group, to be self-assured and physically coordinated enough to toss his or her hat onto that peg across the room then catch the beer being simultaneously tossed from the kitchen with a single hand. These subtleties are the trademarks of cool: that Elvis half-smile, the Fonzie finger snap, Brando's fingers smoothing back his tousled hair—what some refer to as habits of confidence. These habits interact seamlessly with any given social structure—there exists a kind of hum between the cool one and his or her environment. Unfortunately, for the geek, that hum is often a clank.

The Emo

If geeks and nerds are guilty of mind-blindness (not perceiving the thoughts and feelings of others) then emos (who care intensely about the thoughts and feelings of others), could be categorized as over-empathetic hyper-minds. While the geek is slaying monsters on EverQuest, emos are most likely spilling their guts out on MySpace. The term emo derives from the Indy music bands of 1990s Seattle whose lead singers were known to burst into histrionic displays of anxiety, depression, and suicidal heartbreak. More recently, artist like Avril Lavigne have launched the emo archetype into the mainstream. The classic emo is deeply concerned with appearance and fashion trends. The right-brained domains of art, poetry, music, and love are where the emo lives. So, does this mean all emos are cool? No, it just means that when an emo *is* uncool, the emo knows it severely and painfully, which can make an insecure, uncool emo that much uncooler.

But what about those uber cool artist types: the Kerouacs, the Hemingways. Well, Kerouac drank himself to death, and Hemingway, he streamlined the process by simply shooting himself in the head. Artists, in fact, are three times more likely to end up institutionalized than your average slob. The emo who walks into a party picks up on social cues all right, but he also tunes into the horrendous décor, the goddamn car alarm going off outside, *and* the smelly sponge festering on the kitchen counter. Imagine a rare, temperamental orchid planted on the fiftieth yard line of a football field—this is how the artist feels.

While the geeks have been basking in their recent surge in popularity, the emos, conversely, have come under fire. Gerard Way of My Chemical Romance detests the label. In a recent interview, Way stated: "I think emo's a pile of shit."[21] The negative stereotype looks something like this: the tortured emo lives in a suicidal black world of self-imposed misery. Due to gross insecurity, matters of style (hair, clothing, iPod model and placement) are critical to the cynical, melodramatic, emo freak. The urban diction-ary has over 1,000 definitions posted for emo, and most of them are nothing short of death threats. Do the artsy kids really deserve such a bad rap? Some believe that it's the geeks (after surviving years of ridicule) who've launched this anti-emo smear campaign into the blogosphere. Others contend that emo bashing is a self-imposed phenome-non—emos eating their own self-effacing kind. Either way, the tortured right-brained emo may be guilty of little more than trying too hard. Though, in the annals of youth cul-ture, few faux pas breed more contempt than the transparent quest for cool. So:

"An emo walks into a party and . . . all the other emos point and laugh."

Or, maybe the gesture is slightly less obvious or, as in several examples below, as easy to read as a pointed gun. Let's take a look at some common social cues that might fly right over the common geek's head, yet drive the average emo crazy.

Social Cue Comparisons

The forefinger point (at YOU).

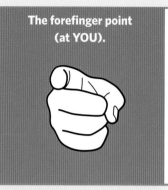

Emo:
Fuck you too.

Geek:
Thank you for acknowledging my wraparound dragon t-shirt.

The eyeroll.

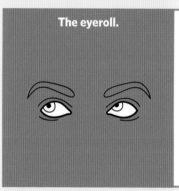

Emo:
What, you like being alive?

Geek:
...as I was saying, a Beastlord is another class of damage dealer...

Prolonged eye contact with parted lips and rapid sultry breathing.

Emo:
You only want to use me then throw me away like the piece of crap I am.

Geek:
Do you want to borrow my inhaler?

Waving arms while screaming FIRE!	**Emo:** Right—I'll find a comfortable seat. **Geek:** Oh—you want to borrow my flameless, rechargeable, USB lighter?

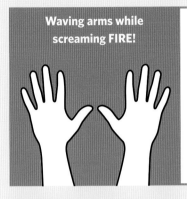

Punch in the face.	**Emo:** You're the only one who understands. **Geek:** So you're not pregnant, just fat?

Hands over mouth with accompanying scream.	**Emo:** It's my breath? God, tell me it's not my breath. **Geek:** Don't tell me—you're into LARPing too!

Geek and Emo: True or False

1. The coin-collectors "carry pack" was invented by world-renowned numismatist, Chris Carrabba, and launched at the 1984 Rare Coin Convention in Hamburg, Germany. His classic design enabled coin enthusiasts to whiz through trade shows, examining and purchasing one-of-kind specimens at record speeds (with both hands!) without the handicaps of the cumbersome backpack. In 1984, the patented design was stolen by New York fashion design firm, Morrissey LTD, and renamed "the Fanny Pack." Within six months, the Fanny Pack became a must-have workout accessory after Morrissey, LTD, shamelessly promoted it (along with matching headbands) in Olivia Newton John's *Physical* video. **True or False?**

2. An anorak is a term used to describe someone who partakes in obsessive hobbies such as pylon- and train-spotting. Anoraks are most often seen beneath electricity pylons or parallel to train tracks with pencils and tiny notebooks in hand. Almost exclusively, the Anorak favors the grey or green nylon snorkel jacket with fur-trimmed hood. *Look at that poor anorak, all alone, peeking out of his telescopic hood.* **True or False?**

3. Bob Bryer, of the band My Chemical Romance, was hospitalized for "physical exhaustion and emotional distress" while filming *Famous Last Words*. Bryer later commented that the video set "brought up a lot of, you know, bad childhood shit." **True or False?**

4. Polyhedral dice are used by Shadow Knights in the virtual casinos of the Galactic Republic. Shadow Knights are given free drinks at the RavensLord craps tables whereby each knight is expected to strip a piece of armor for every roll he loses. Winner knights are allotted entry keys to The RavensLord penthouses and permitted "free rolls" with cocktail waitress-maidens. **True or False?**

5. The band Fugazi tried to prevent price gouging of their fan base by keeping the price of their concert tickets below ten dollars. The band also discouraged violent behavior and aggressive slam dancing. To prevent further displays of raw frustrated emotion, the bouncers carried envelopes of ten-dollar bills which they refunded to the power slammers as they were escorted from the show. **True or False?**

6. All over the country, thousands of rogues, fire demons, and sorcerers gather to LARP in available fields and parks. There, dressed in elaborate medieval garb, they battle the forces of evil, but mostly one another, with foam axes, swords, hammers, and crossbows. **True or False?**

7. Matchbook Romance is headlined by identical twin brothers who simultaneously shaved their heads and removed all body piercings to protest the unethical practice of industrialized pig farming. **True or False?**

8. A berserker is a term used to describe the psychologically distraught state of a Mac user who is forced (often by unsuspecting employers) to convert to the less intuitive PC Windows operating system. *While temping, Dave lost his shit looking for the system-preference tab. Finally, he pulled a berserker and pounded the keyboard with his Ninja Turtle lunchbox.* **True or False?**

9. After receiving the renowned "Hawthorne Award" for designing the highly regarded Masters of the Universe mini-statues, Sylvia Plath turned her talents to the NCCA (National Crossword Competition of America) winning first place in both 2004 and 2005. **True or False?**

10. Otaku is a term used to describe the controversial yet wildly popular sport of Dwarf Rolling whereby "little people" are rolled down steep hills in an attempt to knock down large inflatable bowling pins. *Otaku is disgusting, I can't believe man's injustice to littler man.* **True or False?**

▶ If you got 3 or more *even* answers correct and the rest wrong, your brain may operate in a more linear, analytical fashion. In other words, you're left-brained with at least some geek tendencies.

▶ If you got 3 or more *odd* answers correct and the rest wrong, your brain may operate in an intuitive, aesthetically driven fashion. In other words, you're right-brained with at least some artistic emo qualities.

▶ If you got six or more both *odd and even* answers correct *or* incorrect you might fall into the increasingly rare brain type known as neurotypical. This unusual variety of brain is not skewed left or right, and refuses to be clumped into stereotypes of any kind.

It is no doubt an oversimplification to deem the right-brained emos and the left-brained geeks. Brain science is far more complicated than left and right. But the medical community has made recent discoveries that are helping neurologists understand how deficiencies in particular areas of the brain can lead to limited social skills. Yes, believe it or not, there *are* tests more conclusive for diagnosing brain types than the True and False test you just took. You can even go to one of the recent chains of brain-imaging centers (check your local mall) and, for a few thousand dollars, get your brain scanned. This type of scan is called a SPECT (Single Photon Emission Computed Tomography) and it can identify any number of neurological conditions by measuring blood flow to different areas of the brain.

The Caltech Cool Study

A similar technology to SPECT, called fMRI imaging, has made it possible for scientists to scan the brain's reaction to specific stimuli. Steven Quartz, head of Caltech's Social Cognitive Neuroscience Lab, recently directed a fMRI study on brains and cool which was featured in an article in *Wired Magazine.* To begin the process, subjects were shown 140 images all previously rated by Quartz on a coolness scale from 0 to 5. He then documented which brain area reacted (and with what intensity) to these cool or uncool images. The subject's reactions were then compiled and classified into one of three subsets: High Cool (trendsetters), High Uncool (aware but socially anxious) and the least cool of all, Low Cool or the dreaded Cool Blind—those with little or no reaction at all. Supposedly, the brains of High Cools would light up in response to images like Beyoncé. Alternatively, the brains of Low Cools would light up in response to uncool images like a Ford Escort.

But the Caltech study had problems. Self-admitted geeks and lifelong nerds were scoring uncanny High Cools. Socially adept hipsters, on the other hand, were tallying in as Cool Blind. The stumped researchers finally had to redefine the subsets. High Cool became "Cool Fools" because their brains reacted so intensely to

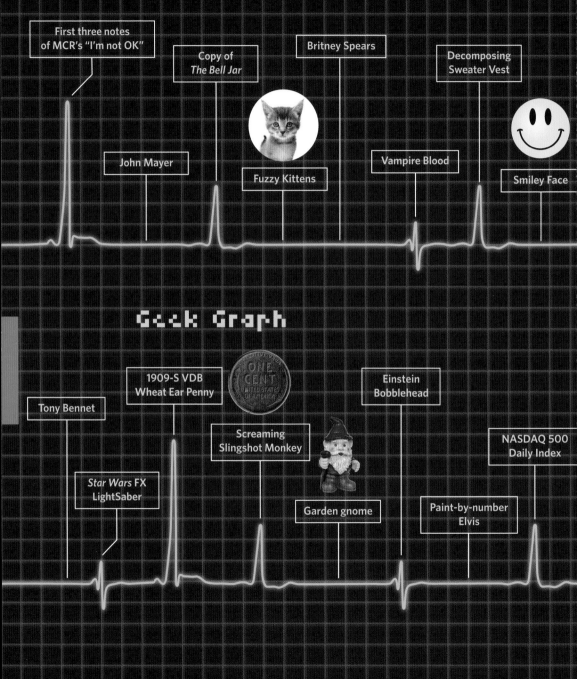

Emo Graph

First three notes of MCR's "I'm not OK"

Copy of *The Bell Jar*

Britney Spears

Decomposing Sweater Vest

John Mayer

Fuzzy Kittens

Vampire Blood

Smiley Face

Geek Graph

1909-S VDB Wheat Ear Penny

Einstein Bobblehead

Tony Bennet

Screaming Slingshot Monkey

NASDAQ 500 Daily Index

***Star Wars* FX LightSaber**

Garden gnome

Paint-by-number Elvis

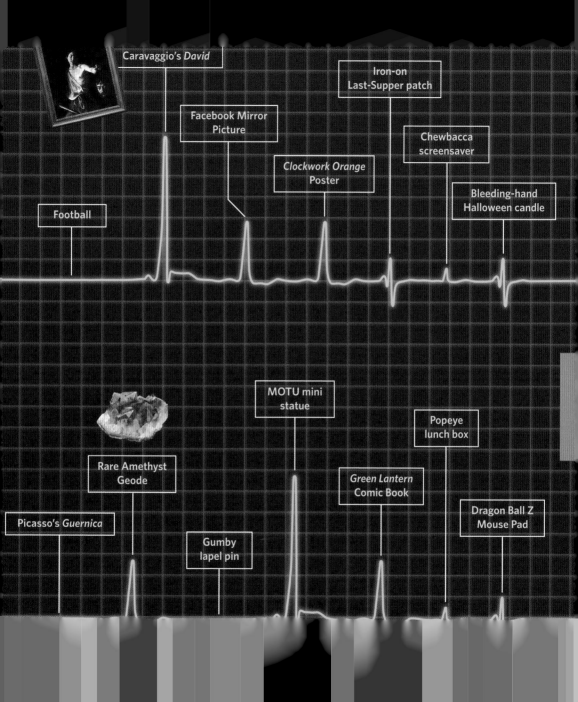

Caravaggio's *David*

Iron-on
Last-Supper patch

Chewbacca
screensaver

Facebook Mirror
Picture

Bleeding-hand
Halloween candle

Clockwork Orange
Poster

Football

MOTU mini
statue

Popeye
lunch box

Rare Amethyst
Geode

Green Lantern
Comic Book

Dragon Ball Z
Mouse Pad

Picasso's *Guernica*

Gumby
lapel pin

cool images like Beyoncé—a subset prone to shop for cool because they did not possess it innately. High Uncool became "Uncool Connoisseurs" because they reacted to uncool images such as Barbra Streisand and Michael Bolton. Low Cools were renamed "Risk-Takers" because these subjects were so worldly that they had virtually no reaction to the images placed before them. In other words, Low Cools were so cool, they were oblivious to outside influence. The fiasco of this Caltech study could have been a study unto itself: "The Scientific Impossibilities of Diagnosing Cool." As the *Wired Magazine* writer who covered the Caltech story (Jennifer Kahn) points out, a test with such tentative results is known, in the scientific community, as a problem of insufficient controls.[22] The research was based on too many ambiguities (*is* Michael Bolton uncooler than Barbra Streisand . . . *is* Beyoncé cooler than a Ford Escort?) The results only illustrate cool's primary characteristic—its essence is its mystery.

Beyoncé

Not Beyoncé

Of course, maybe you don't identify with either the geeks or the emos. In popular culture, notions of cool tend to be closely linked to the creative realms of art (theater, poetry, fashion, music, literature). Historically, there may be more famously cool artistic types than there have been famously cool scientific types. Primarily, this is because artistic types are often in the entertainment limelight anyway: Marlene Dietrich, James Dean, Marlon Brando, to name a few. Film stars have a distinct advantage over geeks when it comes to defining cool—namely exposure on those larger than life movie screens. It takes a lot for a geek to become famously cool. Take Einstein for example. His trademarked name has been applied to numerous "intellectual" products; his image is everywhere from Beatles album covers (*Sgt. Pepper*) to "Think Different" billboards (Apple). Mariah Carey even titled an entire album "$E=MC^2$." How did Einstein go from mega-brain professor to red-hot merchandizing tool? Yes he was brilliant, but it was the man's eccentricity and steadfast original thinking that won the hearts of the world.

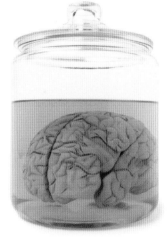

Atypical Brains?

Einstein's brain, if scientists could scan it today, would probably not test as neurotypical. The neurotypical is what sociologists use as their benchmark for average: its learning style is 37% hapatic (moving, touching, doing), 34% auditory (speech, music) and 29% visual (pictures).[23] Whether or not neurotypicals are becoming an extinct brain species depends upon which neuroscientist you talk to. Everyone it seems, from kindergarteners to teenagers to grandma, is being diagnosed with atypical brains. To some, this might feel like a badge of honor, to others, a disapproving label. Yet atypicals are finding each other and celebrating their weirdness as never before. Numerous specialized dating websites are hotbeds for reproductive activity, everything from Emo Love to Geek 2 Geek. The tendency is called positive assortative mating. In nature, it brings same-species individuals with similar characteristics together. For example, turquoise-breasted fu fu birds may seek out mates that are more green than blue. Ultimately, a green-breasted fu fu species is born. In humans this "likes attract" tendency may be responsible for excessively tall Norwegians, passionate Italians, and the Geek explosion in Silicon Valley.

Fortunately, many opposites do still attract and when they do, it's called negative assortative mating. Trait variance is very important to the health of a species, which is why so many Royals, after mating with their cousins, gave birth to insane hemophiliacs. Lack of trait variance is also why puppy mills and backyard breeders are creating purebred dogs who can't breathe with sad little wagons strapped onto their withered hind legs. Mutts are always the healthiest and most well-adjusted of the dog-park crowd (and that includes the people). Without atypical brains there would be no opposites to be attracted *to*.

Brain-type variation gives birth to those eccentricities that the neurotypicals find oh-so-alluring. In other words, those atypical brains are often the ones to unwittingly break the current molds and start something new. Cool itself transcends all labels: geek, emo, nerd, starving artist . . . even hipster. Einstein's brain was no doubt better at quantum physics than it was at picking out a tie; but could he have had a little emo mixed in with his geek? It was the Einstein riding his bike, sticking out his tongue; the Einstein that even Marilyn Monroe thought was sexy—this was what made him an icon of cool.

It All Comes Down to Sex

What creatures won't do to attract a mate of the opposite sex. At its core, cool may be less about mystique and more about basic reproductive science. Here is where the phenomenon of cool starts getting a little transparent. The joke might go like this:

> Why did the chicken cross the road in leather pants?
> To have sex with the chickens on the other side.

The chickens, of course, are men, women, zebras, goats, toads, squid; even grasshoppers need to get it on. And there is no greater aphrodisiac than cool. In humans, cool acquires more sex than brute physical force does, plus, it's easier on the conscience. Imagine if all sexual activity involved an arduous high-speed chase—there would be no juju left over for the real thing. It also has to do with hierarchy: the cooler you are the more partners you have to choose from. In fact, why chose at all? Just have sex with them all. This is what any number of mammals do. A dominant male silverback gorilla can have up to thirty females at his beck and call. It's true, some guys do get all the babes. Of course, this "winner gets all" system breeds a lot of frustrated not-so-lucky males. Unlucky male tortoises have been known to hump rocks all day. Unlike many of our fellow mammals, it's not always the biggest, meanest, and most dominant that come out on top. A lot of fat, nasty men are not getting laid no matter what kind of sports car they drive. Yet, as long as a guy has cool appeal, he can be "short, sweet, even broke, and he'll still be having lots of sex. The Fonz was only 5'6". So, who gets lucky? In Giant Tortoise land, it's the one with the longest neck. Down at the nightclub, it's the one with all the cool.

Mating Comparisons

What is fashion if not an attempt to look hotter for the opposite sex? All our adornments are really no different than a peacock's tail or a robin's red breast. If you think our human obsession with appearance is the least bit misguided—think again. We couldn't be more predictable, at least scientifically. No matter how strange the fashion, Nature already has a mating habit to rival its outlandishness. The truth is, we're all desperate to get noticed. It's a jungle out there, and not just metaphorically. We're competing for sex the minute we walk out the door, partnered or not—and this instinct is what motivates us to look and be looked at. Let's zoom in on nature and see if we don't just see ourselves.

Booty Call of the Amazon

When female baboons are in estrus and ready to mate, their rear ends swell up and turn bright red. They then bend over and "present" their fabulous asses to male baboons—just in case they hadn't already noticed. At the zoo, women might cringe at these repulsive red asses . . . yes, all the while leaning over the railing in front of the baboon exhibit in their skin tight booty shorts (you know, the ones with the word "JUICY" scrawled from cheek to cheek). Ass fashion has reached a zenith over the past decade—so much attention showered onto the booty. It's been branded with rhinestones, tattooed, and garnished with thong antennae. Booty shakin' contests are as common as spelling bees. Presenting *the ass*, starring *the ass*—now showing everywhere!

Welcome to My Crib

While most women are not really impressed with sectional leather sofas, gigantic flat-screen TVs, and faux zebra skin rugs, men are somehow under the impression that they are. A man's home, as the saying goes, is his castle, and behemoth castles are better than quaint cozy castles. The male bowerbird is known as the master builder. McMansions have nothing on this little stud. He spends a tremendous amount of his life-energy building and decorating his bachelor pad. His own coloring is drab, no spectacular feathers or headdresses, but he makes up for it with real estate. The huge structure he builds, made essentially of twigs, is obsessively decorated with stones, feathers, berries and flowers, all meticulously arranged in monochromatic themes. It even has a yard. And if another bowerbird's pad is more interesting than his own? No problem, the bowerbird just steals what he likes. Talk about lawn envy.

 VS.

Nice Package

Not everyone can have a package the size of a cucumber like Robert Plant. Male silverback gorillas can weigh in at five hundred pounds, but their manhood is only one-and-a-half inches long. An intimidating enough physique can get away with a modest endowment. The male argonaut octopus, on the other hand, is about twenty times smaller than the female. If that weren't bad enough, in order to mate with big mamma, the tiny guy's penis has got to actually detach—that's right, come *off*, and swim its little penis self inside her. Back in the days when men wore leotards they were particularly concerned with the size of their package, and rightly so because there *it* was (or wasn't) for all to see. Thus, the practice of wearing a codpiece became standard. These cup-shaped covers were often contoured and abundantly padded to enhance the genitalia. Let's just say that *every* man looks good in a codpiece. Nature has come up with its own ways to draw attention to the penis. The Argentine lake duck is just seventeen inches long—and so is its penis. Now that's a package no female can miss. But if the female duck, by any chance, does fail to notice, the penis reaches out and lassoes her in for action.

Dance Moves

Ah, the ubiquitous male dance solo, from *Saturday Night Fever* to *Dirty Dancing* to *Napoleon Dynamite*. Is there anything finer in the natural world? Actually there is. The manakin bird is so cool, he moonwalks for the ladies. The little fellow can slide backward up to three feet with his skinny bird legs completely straight. Flamingos, cockatiels, sandhill cranes, prairie chickens, musk ducks, birds of paradise, and peacocks are just some of the species that put on flamboyant displays in hopes of attracting a female's attention. A lekking display is a formalized competitive event in the animal kingdom where males go out and strut their stuff, one after the other. Other scientifically confirmed lekking arenas are: Bally's weight rooms, beaches with tiki bars, Burning Man interpretive dance circles, and every light-up dance floor.

Are Those Real?

There is not a lot of difference between Pamela Anderson's surgically enhanced breasts and a mating frigatebird's cherry-red inflatable chest. This little guy's balloon of love blows up to half his body size. The female gelada baboon has a red, hairless, cleavage-shaped patch of skin on its chest. As mentioned earlier, most primates "present" with their rear ends, yet the gelada baboon forages for food sitting down, so most of the day, her ass is out of view. The chest, in this case, offers higher visibility—like a billboard on a highway as opposed to a dead end street. Breast implants, while an excellent means of stopping traffic, suffer the curse of trying too hard. As such, they may appear abnormal, which, in the mating game, can be critically off-putting. And yes, it's easy to tell because most women with breast implants display them like bowling trophies. Imagine the frigatebird hooked up to an air pump: think other birds would notice? But authentically big hooters? Now these are scientifically proven assets to the human mating game, as there is no other reason for breasts to be fat and round (a shape which ironically, only makes breastfeeding more difficult). The primate's relatively flat breast with elongated nipples is a far better design for the infant to get milk. Many scientists believe that the breast became the new presenting butt because humans have sex front to front.

VS.

The Frustrated Bachelor

Nothing is scarier than a gang of angry, sexually frustrated men. Some anthropologists believe this is the root of all war. When a guy isn't getting enough, he tends to surround himself with a bunch of other guys who also aren't getting enough, a phenomenon known in nature as "the bachelor group." Bachelor groups are most common in polygynous social structures where one dominant male lives and wards over a much larger group of females and their young. The other, not-so-lucky males are essentially kicked out of the harem. These bachelor groups often adopt a mob mentality, with hell-raising their number-one pastime. Bachelor elephant seals have been reported to rape female harbor seals, and because the elephant seal is ten times bigger, he often kills her in the process (death by flubber). There is also evidence of bachelor males bullying and occasionally killing young defenseless pups of their own species. In humans, the angry mob can be just as ugly. Cool is never found in bully gangs. Why? Because the genuinely cool (who are always getting enough) have nothing to prove.

The Science of Cool: Conclusion

For those about to dance: we salute you. And to all of you who have, from the Lindy Hoppers of the Apollo Ballroom to the lekking circles of Brooklyn discos, from the lone Burning Man hippie trapped inside his invisible wall to the talent-show break dancer, we thank you for your courage. Your cool was at stake but you persevered. Why? For the sake of sex, and what better reason to dance like a jerk? Yes, some dance better than others and maybe the reason is genetic. We may never know why every Christmas party has a dancing Elaine and why that Elaine is always white, just like we may never know if Groundhog Day is a legitimate barometer of the coming spring. Brain science, though—now this is a valid field of study. The brains of geeks really do look different than the brains of their hyper artistic brethren. But cool, this is much harder to isolate, like nailing that moment when a word, repeated over and over, becomes and indecipherable unword. These are ephemera no scientist can test for; in fact, as the Caltech cool study attests, these are things that make scientists want to beat artists over the head with textbooks. However, this won't stop the designers, marketers, and advertisers, because isolating cool is worth billions in sales. The following section takes a hard numbers look at the ever-expanding business of cool.

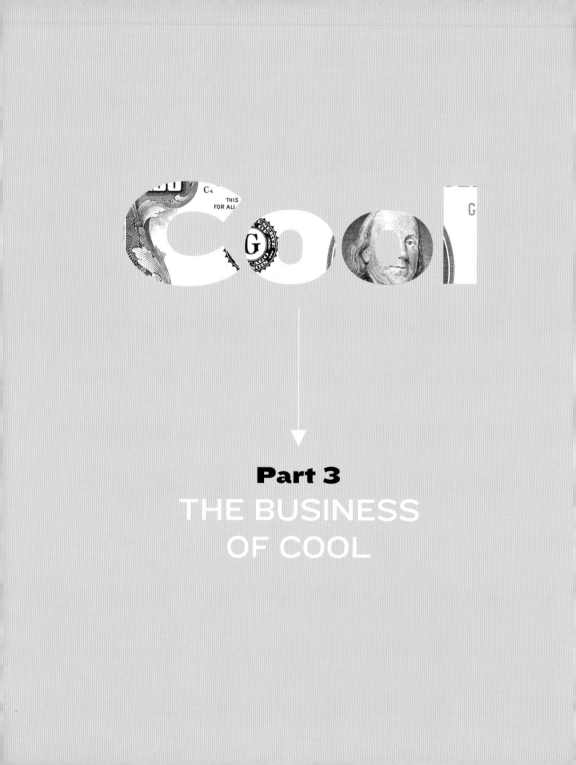

Part 3
THE BUSINESS
OF COOL

The Business of Cool: Introduction

No one wants to be deemed uncool, and this premise has earned advertisers billions. Some even claim that uncool was invented by Madison Avenue right along with panty lines, halitosis, and white underarm residue. Is cool really getting hijacked by corporate America as a means to sell logo-ridden products to insecure teens? Well, the numbers speak for themselves: corporate America spends over three billion dollars a year on advertising targeted to teens. Teens, in turn, spend over 200 billion dollars a year on stuff that's cool.[1] And that's just the teens; throw in the rest of us and the numbers climb into the trillions. Globally, advertisers spend at least 500 billion a year persuading us to buy their products.[2] The onslaught is so relentless, the average schlump sees more ads in a single year than people 50 years ago saw in their entire lifetime. Visual clutter is, no doubt, at an all-time high, with the message-makers clamoring for your eyeballs like never before. The cycle of modern commerce will continue to churn as long as consumers are willing to empty their wallets. And we are. Want, it seems, can be manufactured—not unlike a cheese. Just follow the recipe, let ferment, and voilà. This part of the book examines the science of Want: how the advertisers compel us to spend by tapping into our universal insecurities (fear + want = buy). The fear of getting left behind might be attributed to the bandwagon effect—the mechanism that kicks in to create a fad. Although, as much as advertisers might like us to believe it, fresh breath and skinny jeans never made anyone cool. But hey (and this is what they count on), it's a start isn't it?

Does all this advertising mean the fashion industry is more aggressive today than it was in its infancy? How are the red-carpet gowns of the Academy Awards really any different from those on the grand boulevards of seventeenth-century Paris? While Haute Couture may still influence fashion, your typical consumer does not consult Versace's fall line before shelling out for a new pair of jeans. How, then, does one decide which pair of jeans to buy? Rather than setting the fashion standards as the Haute Couture houses of old, today's clothing industry claims to look towards the streets, to the people themselves, for inspiration. The hunt is on, and the company that discovers the next cutting-edge trend will cash in big. Cool is the Holy Grail, and Madison Avenue will stop at nothing in their never-ending quest for it. "Coolhunters" are corporate America's latest invention: hired culture spies, combing the streets for the next potential fad. In the end though, how much of this "street inspired" fashion really comes from the people first? In other words, are the fashion and music industries giving the people what they want—or *telling* the people what to want? This section of the book will examine that very question, while revealing a few of the coolhunt's more subversive tactics.

Haute Couture

Paris in the mid seventeenth-century was considered the epicenter of high fashion, and everyone who was anyone had their dresses custom designed, fitted, and sewn by one of the few select fashion houses. Designer Charles Frederick Worth is considered the granddaddy of Haute Couture. He made his fame designing elaborate "presentation dresses" which affirmed a young debutante's status as she came out into society. The better the dress, the better the husband she could hope to snare. At the time Paris had an emerging affluent class, eager to show off their newly acquired wealth. To answer this demand, a thriving economy in luxury goods was born. Haute Couture was fashion for the upper crust, as a single dress could cost twenty times the average tradesman's annual salary. This was excess and conspicuous consumption in its heyday: Marie Antoinette sported dresses that were three times her actual size and pompadour hairstyles that took teams of coiffeurs days to create. Haute Couture still exists today, and conspicuous consumption is alive and well. With money to burn, the affluent still look to the fashion authorities to confirm their social status. The Scott Henshall diamond-encrusted dress worn by Samantha Mumba to the 2004 premiere of *Spiderman II* was priced at approximately nine million dollars.[3] Only a few of the finest designer houses meet the criteria to be couture approved. In fact, the name Haute Couture itself is legally protected to insure against use by unworthy, bottom-feeding designers. Recently, the Haute Couture designer, Fendi, sued Wal-Mart for allegedly counterfeiting their handbags, selling them for a mere $295, compared with the $925 Fendi version.[4]

Marie Antoinette: dressed to excess

Any woman who wears a couture gown to the Academy Awards, can rest assured that no one else will be wearing one quite like it. Yet in time, dozens of knockoffs will be manufactured in homage to her one-of-a-kind fashion statement. So the couture client not only buys that original exclusivity but also the privilege of initiating a particular look, in short "owning a trend." The plunging Versace gown made famous at the 2000 Grammy Awards by Jennifer Lopez was knocked off ad infinitum. Jennifer's risqué V-neck dropped all the way

Jennifer Lopez: queen of "vevage"

down past her navel, making breast "vevage" a standard cut of prom gown fashions for years to come.

Haute Couture may still lay claim to the red-carpet market, but 99.999 percent of fashion is now manufactured with the masses in mind. Gone are the days when ladies of leisure settled onto their divans to enjoy drawing-room fashion shows. *Pret-a-porter* means ready-to-wear and it is here, at the lower end of the fashion market, where the big profits live.

The Coolhunters

Let's say you're a large corporation, and, like most large corporations, you want to make as much money as humanly possible, and fast. Most likely, your target audience will be the demographic known for spending the most money, fast, and that means teens and twenty-somethings. Unfortunately, most of the industry's top-notch art directors are pushing retirement, and while they may be aware that bell bottoms have gone out, come back, and gone back out again, they have no idea what youth culture is currently about. Luckily for you, there are coolhunters for hire—thousands of culture scouts ready to fill you in on the highly coveted secrets of the young and eager to spend. The fashion world is replete with innovative young marketers wanting to sell their street research for big bucks. Some charge as much as $50,000 a year for the simple privilege of logging onto their websites, where compiled Cool can be snatched up—red-hot—and transformed into merchandise.

The coolhunter's mission is to seek out cultural eccentricities, modest blips as opposed to full-fledged trends. The less developed, the better. These fashion oddities are sought out and documented by guerilla photographers who hang out in skateboard parks, boardwalks, and other teen venues famous for daredevil posers. Let's say for example, some kid wears one knee sock and one ankle sock by accident. A coolhunter might zone in on this potential trend, now only in its zygote stage. High-low-sock-kid happily poses for the coolhunter's camera, thrilled to have his genius finally acknowledged for the sort of oversight his mother usually rewards with a rolled-up newspaper to the side of his head. The hope, then, is for the coolhunters to bring their clandestine anthropological research to the large corporation, possibly suggesting this "high-low-sock-thing" as the next no-miss investment.

The Life Cycle of a Fad

"Fashion is nothing but an induced epidemic."

▶ **George Bernard Shaw**

Is high-low-sock-kid really part of the sacred two to three percent of what those in the industry refer to as innovators? Next come the trendsetters, according to Sharon Lee of Look-Look (a top coolhunting operation), tallying in around seventeen percent. Trendsetters may zero in on something the innovator does and copy it, often claiming to have invented it themselves. An early adaptor is one of the brave few to take that still-odd-thing into the vast eighty percent of the mainstream.[5] The odd thing, once captured by the merchandiser, soon becomes a fad, then a common thing, and finally an uncool dead thing. As a rule, that fad (if the merchandisers catch the wave in time) rakes in big capital. How big depends on what it is, how much it costs to produce, and how much people are willing to pay for it. If your product is quick enough to market, there may be no competition to drive revenues down. Timing here, is everything.

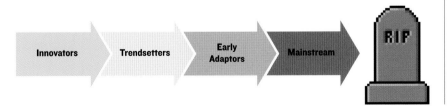

Catching the Wave

Jump in too soon, and the wave rushes directly overhead; too late, it's entirely missed. The term "jumping the shark" is used, most often, to describe the tipping point when a sitcom officially dies. The original expression is a reference to the *Happy Days* episode when the water skiing Fonzie (Henry Winkler) jumps the shark. (This syndrome was parodied on *Arrested Development* in a scene where Henry Winkler jumps over a dead shark.) In essence, this necessary death occurs when writers and producers try too hard to save that which is already gasping for air. Other examples include Nancy Reagan as a "very special guest" on *Different Strokes*, or the "flaming helicopter" episode on *ER*. But jumping the shark is not limited to sitcoms; any trend can do it. The challenge to those out there trying to cash in is, how fast, how much, and . . . when is it too late to bother?

Once the bets are placed, the advertising and manufacturing begins. Sales forecasts must be dead-on or big profits end up down the crapper, as was the case with the great Tickle Me Elmo shortage of 1996. In days of old, consumer demand came first, then production followed. Today's markets have no patience for such unprofitable dead time. These days, an advertiser's job is to manufacture want, first and foremost. This way, a product is already red-hot before it's launched into the marketplace. Ideally, consumer demand is directly in step with production. If this formula strays too far out of sync, the over-produced item may end up lingering for years in last-chance dollar bins. Of course, while want can be created, it's far from the exact science that merchandisers bank on. Fads are often transient, existing in mysterious realms of their own making. But the rewards of taming the beast of cool-appeal are too great, and therefore, youth-centric companies like Viacom will never give up the quest.

With so many uncontrollable factors at play, capitalizing on the next big fad is as easy as forecasting the path of next year's killer hurricane. Simply telling people what to want is so much easier than predicting what they *might* want. While the cool scouts out there might be busy taking the pulse of youth culture, there's not much evidence that CEOs are using this data to give kids what they really want. Sure, kids want to be cool, but they also want advertisers to stop telling them *what's* cool. This contradiction is the Achilles heel of teen culture and this is why, like it or not, Madison Avenue now claims to be the authority on cool. Teens are very impulsive, and therefore highly exploitable creatures. Large corporations are in the position (financially and strategically) to colonize the teen media landscape—radio, television, movies, magazines, video games, even chatrooms. Penetrate enough media with incarnations like Hannah Montana and Lizzie McGuire and they'll be *cool enough* to sell millions in merchandise.

No-Profit Wonders

Rarely, a fad comes along with virtually little or no commercial value. The best examples may be flagpole sitting and streaking. Flagpole sitting was big from 1924 to 1929. Initiated by a dare, a guy named Alvin Kelly sat on ass-sized platforms, which were fixed to the top of various flagpoles, for days on end. His record—49 days—was set atop an Atlantic City flagpole in 1929. That year, kids all over America partook in this curious non-sport. Baltimore alone claimed at least twenty pole-sitting youths, their family and friends cheering them on.[6] Sixty-nine years later, a guy name Harvey Danger wrote a song called "Flagpole Sitta" which was a nominal success in 1998, but other

than this, little actual capital was generated by the practice of pole sitting. Imagine the austere feat of pole sitting caught up in today's insatiable market. Such potential. Can you say, memory-foam-cushioned, magic-finger massaging, turbo-heated, MONSTER-ASS POLE SEAT (with optional beverage holder and reading light)?

Streaking was another no-profit wonder. An unlikely amalgam of flashing and jogging, this exhibitionist fad became commonplace at 1970s sporting events. Soon students everywhere were streaking across campus quads. A few streak-centric products were produced in an attempt to cash in on the fad: buttons, a wristwatch featuring a streaking Nixon, pink underwear that read "Too Shy to Streak," a song by Ray Stevens which featured the lyric "always making the news wearing just his tennis shoes." Yet all in all, streaking, by its minimalist nature, was a veritable loser in the novelty market. Again, it wasn't until 2004 that market savvy Nike resurrected the old fad to sell the only obvious thing a naked jogger could need: streaker sneakers, in this case the Nike "Shox."

Pole sitting and streaking aside, your average fad means big revenues for the company lucky enough to bring it to market first. The following fads generated enough economic buzz to inspire the early retirement of any number of CEOs— off they went, bonus checks in hand, to build garish tropical McVillas. The profits varied, depending on the fad, but often rivaled the GDP of many smaller countries. Let's take a look at some fads and their undocumented best-guess statistics.

★　★　★

Ten Little Fads That Could

Saddle Shoes innovated 1955

Who Made Out: Spalding, Inc.

Hallmark Moment: Elvis wears them in Jailhouse Rock

Demise: Killed by hippie Jesus sandal

Lasting Impression: Schoolgirl fetish must-have

Ouija Boards initiated late 60s

Who Made Out: Kenneth Fuld of Kennard (Fuld eventually sold rights to Parker Bros.)

Hallmark Moment: 1973 *Exorcist*—Megan communicates with Captain Howdy

Demise: Still magically appears at fifth grade sleepover parties

Lasting Impression: Grandma, is that you?

Sea-Monkeys initiated 1972

Who Made Out: Harold Von Braunhut

Hallmark Moment: In 1975, sea-monkeys were advertised in 80% of all comic books

Demise: Guaranteed within two days

Lasting Impression: What stinks in here?

The Pet Rock innovated 1975

Who Made Out: Ad Executive Gary Dahl

Hallmark Moment: Gary Dahl appears on *The Tonight Show*

Demise: Put to sleep in 1976

Lasting Impression: Son-of-a-bitch rock cost me four bucks

Chia Pet innovated 1982

Who Made Out: Joseph Enterprises, Inc

Hallmark Moment: Mr. "T" Chia Pet introduced in 2000 on Conan O'Brian show

Demise: Re-sprouts annually under three out of four American Christmas trees

Lasting Impression: Can you say verdurous covering?

Reebok Pump innovated 1989

Who Made Out: Marketing expert Mark Goldston

Hallmark Moment: Dee Brown pumping up for NBA Slam Dunk

Mortality: Dead by mid-90s due to questionable inflatable bladder technology

Lasting Impression: $175.00 clown shoes

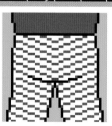

Zubaz pants innovated 1991

Who Made Out: Bodybuilders Dan Stock and Bob Truax

Hallmark Moment: Road Warriors endorsement

Demise: Introducing Zubaz diapers!

Lasting Impression: Ferrari substitute for the mulleted tailgater

The Rachel-from-*Friends* Cut innovated mid-90s
Who Made Out: The Sedu, manufacturer of the flat hair iron
Hallmark Moment: "I'm over you, Ross."
Demise: Still lingering in New Jersey junior high schools
Lasting Impression: The trampy un-perm

The Furby born 1998
Who Made Out: Tiger Electronics
Hallmark Moment: "Desperate Parents Injured in Furby Toy Store Stampede!"
Demise: Birth of Hasbro's Gizmo
Lasting Impression: U-nye-loo-lay-foo = Please don't smash me with that hammer.

Crocs initiated 2002
Who Made Out: Crocs, Inc, Boulder, Colorado
Hallmark Moment: Sported by Iron Chef Mario Batali on the cover of *Sporting News*
Demise: Confirmed dead in 2007 when George W. Bush is photographed in black crocs.
Lasting Impression: #6 worst on Maxim's 2007 "The 10 Best and Worst Things to Happen to Men" list.

★ ★ ★

Calling the Moment of Death
The Top Five signs that a fad is done for:

1. Third graders have got them, without knowing why.

2. The Party Store now stocks them in the "accessories" aisle.

3. John Stamos is wearing it on TV.

4. A YouTube video surfaces of said item in blender.

5. George W. Bush is wearing them, with socks.

The Science of Want

A student of Socrates once asked him why he bothered coming to the market when he never bought a thing. "I am always amazed to see," Socrates replied, "just how many things there are that I don't need."[7] Yet the difference between need and want is the basis of most first-world economies. Let's say you're a ginormous company with something to sell. You've got the gizmo, it's already been mass-produced overseas and what you need to sell it is buzz. Enough buzz and people will kill for your gizmo—literally kill for it—like the famed Xbox murders. When the game Manhunt was connected (in theory) to the murder of a fourteen-year-old boy, HMV spokesperson Gennaro Castaldo commented, "Interest in Manhunt has significantly increased for all the wrong reasons. It's flying off the shelves."[8] The Manhunt buzz was, of course, unintentional, but it serves to illustrate what exposure—even the most negative exposure—can do for product sales. Short of a murder story, what other tactics might advertisers be hiding in their toolbox these days?

Under the Radar

In *The Tipping Point,* Malcolm Gladwell explains why word of mouth is the most powerful marketing tool there is. Consumers, now seeing upwards of 3,000 ads a day, have burned out on traditional media formats. Besides, who can really trust a paid message? Gladwell contends that "people embrace more primitive social bonds and turn to the very personal networks run by mavens and connectors."[9] The connector is the one who throws the best parties and the maven is always the most interesting person there; people trust them implicitly. If the mavens and connectors love your product, its success is guaranteed. But what if the mavens and connectors of the world fail to acknowledge, much less cheerlead, for your gizmo? It's simple: you infiltrate the system. Here are some ways that companies do precisely that:

▶ **Slumber Party Apprentice:** How about inviting your bestest girlfriends over for a night of crazy séances? No. Boy gossip? No. Levitating the fat girl? No. Popcorn and movies? No. Well then, how about intensive product assessment? A firm called GIA (Girls Intelligence Agency) is looking for "secret agents" to throw parties and use their closest friends as barometers of cool. GIA gives their secret agents boxes of free "cool" stuff. These freebies are evaluated at the slumber party, dispensed to the participants, and hopefully "pre-circulated" all over select junior high schools.

▶ **Chat Room Whore:** Companies like New York's Cornerstone Promotion hire kids to log into chat rooms and other online communities. These paid promoters masquerade as normal people while gushing about the virtues of the *hidden client's* product.

▶ **The Cunning Drop:** With the advent of TiVo and commercial-skipping technology, advertisers are dropping their commercials *inside* the entertainment rather than around it. Sometimes, the product placement is subtle, as in 1982's *ET* (the product was Reese's Pieces). Other times the plot seems to be written around the product, turning the entertainment into more of an infomercial than anything else. *All My Children* was guilty of this in 2002 when it wrote a Revlon cosmetics drama right into the storyline. Movies are rife with in-your-face products and copious shots of car, soda, and every other sort of logo. Even rap and literature has jumped on the brandwagon with products dropped into song lyrics and novel plots.

▶ **Street Spammers:** *Aqua Teen Hunger Force* paid two starving artists $300 to place 40 magnetic light boxes in "hip and trendy areas" throughout Metro Boston. The stunt, in America's post-9/11 climate, set off a bomb scare that cost Boston approximately $500,000.[10] In San Francisco, guerilla marketers were arrested for defacement and fined $100,000 for stenciling "Peace, Love, Linux" on the city's sidewalks.[11] In New York, the Reebok sidewalk painters got off by paying a mere $11,000 dollars.[12] In Austin, a street spammer was also arrested for what one passerby called, "postering the hell out of our city."[13]

▶ **'Sup Man, Can I Buy You a Drink?:** Kirshenbaum Bond & Partners hired 150 actors to hang out in select fashionable nightclubs and bars. The job of these actors was to order the Hennessey Martini as boisterously as possible and buy the special drink for strangers, all the while trumpeting its virtues. The five-year program allegedly increased sales by forty percent.[14]

▶ **Pardon Me, But . . . :** Fathom Communications hired actors to pose as tourists in seven American cities. The fake tourists stopped people on the street asking if they would mind taking their picture. All the "tourists," of course, just happened to be using the T68i cell phone with attachable camera. *The Wall Street Journal* blew the campaign's cover with an exclusive on the stunt. The article was followed by *60 Minutes* expose on Sony and their controversial guerilla marketing tactics.[15]

▶ **Take Our Car ... Please:** Daimler Chrysler gave five brand-new Dodge Durangos to five charities. Other celebrities rumored to "pimp rides" (albeit the environmentally friendly celebrities: after three months of publicity, the cars were auctioned off to BMW Hydrogen 7) are Will Farrell, Brad Pitt, Richard Gere, and Sharon Stone.[16]

▶ **Save Me:** A gorgeous woman whispers "save me" in your ear, slips her phone number into your pocket and disappears. Wow! Only, it's not her number—it's the number for a sales pitch, in this case Majestic, a suspense/thriller game from Electronic Arts.[17]

▶ **Vespa Hotties:** Sunset Place, Melrose, and The Third Street Promenade were a few of the locations these hotties and their Vespas were dispatched to. When approached, the hired actors not only claimed to "love their Vespas," but casually dropped the names of other more famous Vespa hotties like Sandra Bullock and Sisqo.[18]

▶ **Patio Fungus Support Group:** Lucky Strike sent out crews of sympathetic shoulders to cry on for exiled smokers lingering outside office buildings. Offering iced coffee and beach chairs in summer, hot beverages and cell phones in winter, these paid promoters treated the dejected smokers like the priceless Lucky Strike market share they are.[19]

In Your Face

Why bother with subtlety at all? Today, many advertisers opt for the more direct approach of screaming right into the consumers face. These messages are shameless, proud to be wherever you are, even if it *is* a public bathroom. Ads are not only in restrooms, at gas pumps, and on street blimps (big fat billboards on wheels), but they're also on the vertical edges of steps and the bottom of your golf holes. And just in case you weren't paying attention, your train, bus, and entire office building may be wrapped in a half-naked anorexic perfume model. It's a jungle out there and the competition for brand-cool (i.e. market share) is just another process of natural selection—only the fittest survive.

As in nature, good manners are rarely rewarded. The tactics that follow might even send the most tolerant among us running for the media-free hills of Amish country. Companies that employ guerilla and in-your-face marketing flaunt their methods as cutting edge, outside the box, and avant-garde. But does your ad-weary consumer really come to equate these brands with cool—or some insufferable punk whose mouth needs taping shut? The objective is brand recognition at any cost, even if seeing that brand now makes us want to scream. Certainly, the ad that makes feminists froth at the mouth gets noticed. The idiot walking around Times Square with a car ad tattooed onto his forehead gets noticed. Yet in the end . . . does the bully get the girl?

Shock and Awe

Sometimes the advertiser's goal is to metaphorically dope slap you upside the head in an attempt to get its ad noticed amongst the arms race of other ads competing for your attention. The following ads have been known to stupefy even the most oblivious.

▶ **Gucci Pubie:** Gucci recently featured an ad with a standing woman flashing her pubic hair to a man kneeling religiously before her nether-regions. Her pubes are shaved to form the letter "G."[20]

▶ **Dog Breath:** In the U.K. Wrigley's put up a commercial that allegedly caused British children to lose their lunches. In the ad, a guy wakes up with breath so bad that he very graphically vomits up the figurative dog; in this case a slime-soaked terrier. After receiving over 600 complaints, Wrigley's took it off the air.[21]

▶ **Wise-Ass Toilets:** Part of an ABC-TV campaign called for 1,000 speaking billboards to be placed above men's urinals. The witty speaking toilet cracked jokes to urinating men such as: "Oh my God, look at the size of that thing!" and "Hey, watch your shoes!" Another cocky toilet hawking Kozmo rental/delivery services suggested, "That girl's a bitch. Why don't you go home and rent a movie?"[22]

▶ **Oh, Please, Carl:** Carl's Jr. may be most famous for flaunting burger-slut Paris Hilton washing a car, but they've also aired ads that present other burger sluts, one very pornographically riding a bull and another very pornographically wiping down a restaurant table. Another ad for "flat buns" features a slutty teacher's ass, while one for milkshakes showcases a gyrating man suggestively humping a cow with a great set of udders. In 2003 Hugh Hefner, in a documentary-style spot, praised the variety of Carl's Jr.'s menu: "Because some guys don't like the same thing night after night."[23]

▶ **Bennetton, Where's the clothes?:** The most remarkable thing about this clothing retailer's jaw-dropping images of horses having sex, bloody newborn babies, and HIV positive tattoos is their distinct lack of Benetton clothing.

▶ **Oh, shit, it's *Mom!*:** Hebrew National unleashed SUVs packed with promotional "moms." Each "Mom Squad" came equipped with barbecue kits, Frisbees, coupons, and grilling tools. Their mission . . . to expose Hebrew National to the wiener-challenged masses. Rolling across the country, these grilling mavens sniffed out impromptu backyard parties, church bazaars, PTO picnics, and all who refused to drop-kick them back into their monster SUVs. Doing their part for charity, the company donated one pack of their famously nutritious hot dogs (for each

coupon redeemed) to an organization known as "Feeding Children Better."[24]

Captive Audience

There's nowhere to run in the subway, airplane, golf cart, bathroom stall, or taxi, and that's what makes these confined spaces prime advertising real estate. Remember when riding in the elevator meant sharing a claustrophobic space with a gang of unfamiliar office drones? Well, technology has made huge advances in the art of ignoring each other. First the cell phone, then the Blackberry, and now elevator TV. 4,200 video flat screens have now been installed in 400 office buildings. So, rather than letting that standard six elevator minutes per day go to waste, employees can now ride shoulder to shoulder while pharmaceutical giants tout their latest cure-alls for medical ills such as seasonal affective disorder, inflammatory bowel disease, and the dreaded restless leg syndrome.[25]

Body as Billboard

Companies like Toyota have utilized the human forehead for ad space. First, it's relatively cheap; second, it's more versatile than the top of a cab. With temporary tattoos, the branded ones are instructed to make the rounds in high-profile areas like Times Square. Companies like Body Billboardz will even arrange belly, leg, arm, and back rentals for companies wishing to infiltrate these erogenous zones. Andrew Fischer is better known as the "Fore-

head Guy." This 21-year-old began his lucrative advertising career earning $50,000 for leasing out his forehead monthly. It worked out so well that Fischer decided to make himself available on an annual basis; so, the following January, he auctioned his forehead off on eBay. This time the stunt earned only $37,375.[26] Then, Karolyne Smith stepped up to bat; she auctioned off the right to pen a "real" tattoo onto her forehead. Unfortunately for Karolyne, it seemed the real estate bubble had already popped for foreheads, as a company named Goldenpalace.com won the bid for a mere $10,000. Despite objections by the tattoo parlor, Karolyne went ahead and had the company's name, all 15 one-inch-high block letters, eternally inked above her eyebrows.[27] Giving "forehead," it seems, will soon be like giving blood—the dregs of society eager and willing. A Miami start-up called "Lease Your Body" isn't quitting yet; they recruit foreheads for a piddly $100 to $5,000, depending on how good-looking you are.[28] This, in turn, has spurned a new market niche for highly unattractive people who are said to be mobilizing their own eBay campaigns. Soon, corporations will be putting up "hush money" to prevent their logos from showing up on ugly people.

Call Me Mr. FreebeeStore.com

Cody Baker, a US Marine, launched a website, www.choosemyname.com. On it he auctioned off the privilege of being legally renamed by the highest bidder. Mr. Baker's new name would have gone to the highest bidder, Freebiestore.com for $30,000, had the Marines not reminded Mr. Baker that federal law prohibits commercial endorsements by members of the military.[29] Also unlucky was the New York couple, Jason Black and Frances Schroeder, who tried to auction off the naming rights to their newborn son. The bidding started at $500,000. The only patron they would have objected to was a tobacco or gun company. When asked why, Blank replied, "We have our standards." The stunt, of course, was scrutinized by many. "Aren't you concerned about the boy going to school if his name is Scooter Pie?" Mitch Albom asked in an article for the *Los Angeles Business Journal*.[30] Luckily for Junior, he began his life a total loser with no takers on his $500,000 name.

Focus Groups: Please Circle the Coolest

This is what thousands of teens, often recruited in shopping malls and big-box record stores, are asked to do when they agree to participate in focus groups. Kids are usually paid from $50 to $200 for their highly coveted opinions on such critical national issues as "Whose hair would you rather have: Hannah Montana's or Lizzie McGuire's?" Often kids reply with no more than dumbfounded expressions, in which case they must be bribed with sugary treats. Sometimes the stubborn youth are observed like aquarium fish through one-way mirrors and closed-circuit cameras. They reply with rolled eyes and tired expressions as the too-hip group facilitators slip words like "man," "fresh," and "dude" into every other sentence. Focus-group activities often revolve around gut reactions to a wide variety of existing products. Fortunately or unfortunately, dolphin language is often easier to deconstruct than the apathetic mumblings of teens, particularly when it comes to gauging cool. Marketers might be wise to interpret this indifference as message fatigue. Rarely are participants given the opportunity to speak honestly about how the market might serve them better. Rather, they are poked and prodded and surveyed *ad nauseum* on what, when, and how much they are willing to buy.

Marketing Cohorts

Who buys what--this is a big question in the business of cool. What's cool to Uncle Ted may not be so hip to Cousin Sally. In one given family there can exist more than half a dozen marketing cohorts. Are you male, female, black, white, Spanish or Asian? Ancient, old, almost-old, middle-aged, the new forty, thirty-something, eco-boomer undergrad, teen, 'tween, youth, toddler, or infant? Are you poor, not-so-poor, rich, or filthy rich. How about politics? According to a *New York Times* article "Politics on Wheels," (April, 1, 2005) Democrats are 32 to 44 percent more likely to buy a Volvo than a Republican. And old, beat-up Volvos—these are almost exclusively driven by Democrats, while brand new Volvos are appealing to more Republicans than ever before. Hummer buyers, not surprisingly, had a Republican-to-Democrat ratio of 52 to 23. Selling the right stuff to the right people means forgetting all that crap your mother warned you against, like pigeonholing strangers before looking into their hearts or walking a mile in their worn out shoes. Advertisers don't want to waste their precious money advertising teen-centric merchandise via Network News commercials; nor do they want to penetrate Facebook with banner ads for geriatric diapers. "Know your audience" applies here. Cohort research is why porn shops are so often located next to auto parts stores, which men are more likely to frequent alone. Cohorts are also why you might buy one fishing hat for your dad online and receive Trout Digest for the rest of your life. And forget about those catalogs. The more you buy from Amazon, the more accurately your specific tastes can be aligned with buying recommendations. No matter who you are, there is a profile out there to match your forecasted desires.

What's Your Marketing Cohort?

Match the statement below to their target audience.

1. **Early-Adaptor Teen**

2. **Gen X-er**

3. **Nagging Ninja Warrior**

4. **Back-to-School 'Tween**

5. **Trendsetter Teen**

6. **Empty Nesters**

7. **Hyperactive Newlywed**

8. **Pester-powered Princess**

9. **Gen Y-er**

10. **Innovator Teen**

11. **Hypochondrial Gray**

12. **Mainstream Teen**

13. **Suit**

14. **Boomer**

15. **Motorhead 'Burbanite**

A. "We want matching jet skis!"

B. "I want a Paris Hilton lunchbox!"

C. "I invented those damn fuchsia pigtails!"

D. "Oh yeah, I want fuchsia pigtails just like you!"

E. "Let's liquidate our assets and climb Kilimanjaro!"

F. "I love/hate my fucking Blackberry!"

G. "Even Nirvana sucked!"

H. "I am every asshole with fuchsia pigtails!"

I. "That iPod's, like, huge!"

J. "Maybe I do have restless leg syndrome!"

K. "I guess I'll dye my pigtails fuchsia!"

L. "Buy me that sword or I'll kill myself!"

M. "Jim Morrison is too still alive!"

N. "Turbo-powered 4 x 4s pump me up."

O. "Sally says I don't have Barbies 'cuz we're poor."

Answers: 1=K, 2=G, 3=L, 4=B, 5=D, 6=E, 7=A, 8=O, 9=I, 10=C, 11=J, 12=H, 13=F, 14=M, 15=N

Kogals, Cosplay, and Gothic Lolitas

These are names for Japanese fashion types. Young and predominantly urban, this relatively new demographic of women are no longer pressured into early marriages. Kogals have freedom, expensive tastes, and healthy disposable incomes. This cohort is famous for its ability to forecast the success or doom of any given product, particularly electronics. For this reason, Kogals may be a more researched phenomenon than the melting polar ice caps. Their materialistic aesthetic is often compared to that of the California Valley Girl: artificial suntans, dyed blonde hair, and designer handbags. Cosplay, in comparison, is far less conservative. This form of "costume play" is an entire Japanese subculture where people dress up as characters from manga, anime, tokusatsu, and video games. By contrast, Gothic Lolita involves dressing in less outrageous costumes, which are often black or white and Victorian in nature.[31] The extreme styles worn by Gwen Stefani's entourage of Harajuku girls echo all three of these Japanese fashion types.

Mooks and Midriffs

These terms are often used in a derogatory way to describe the lowest common denominator of teen culture. The mook is the fart joke come to life: he's loud, dumb, horny, and smells bad to boot. MTV is famous for their mook programming targeted at teenage boys.[32] The mook is intentionally grotesque, shamelessly sexist, and everywhere boys are. The mook is famous for taking bathroom humor to unsurpassed heights, often partaking in shock-and-awe stunts such as poo-diving and ass waxing. Mooks are also spring-break party animals known for puking on their favorite Vans. Mook show hosts are often guys well into their thirties or forties that remain frozen in perpetual adolescence. A mook's lack of moral conviction makes him a gluttonous consumer and an ideal target audience for any number of products. Madison Avenue loves the mook, but how fair a representation of American manhood is he? A Frontline documentary called *The Merchants of Cool* followed MTV cameras to the house of a randomly selected "average American boy." The goal was to research his buying habits, as well as what makes him tick, sort of a one-on-one focus group between the kid and MTV. If MTV knew what kids really wanted, they would be better able to serve them: at least, this was their claim. Funny thing was the boy they selected was nothing like a mook. He was sweet, shy, the kind of kid who kept his room clean and kissed his mother goodnight. How, then, is MTV serving the real cross section of American boys? Could it be that they are far more interested in telling kids what to want rather than giving them what they really do want?

Midriff is the female counterpart to the mook.[33] She loves the fart jokes, the sexist banter. While the mook is trapped in adolescence, the midriff is brimming with confidence and freakishly mature; in fact, she's so comfortable with her sexuality that she works it like a loaded gun. Every move she makes is so sexually suggestive that she's embarrassing to watch with your mother in the same room. But she's also a bitch and a tease who loves to see men grovel. She could care less about feminism, world peace, or what her mother thinks. But don't call her a bimbo because she's just smart enough to know that men are her puppets. Her sex appeal fills her entire identity; it is her politics, her ticket to ride. Famous midriff Britney Spears often uses porn producers to create her music videos. Again, is the midriff a reasonable portrayal of teenage girls or a marketing persona aimed at selling them merchandise? Want, as corporate moguls have discovered, *can* be programmed, packaged and sold.

Manufactured Celebrity

The concept of manufactured celebrity has been around a good long time (Motown, the Monkees, to name a few of its incarnations). Sure, everyone loved Motown in the 60s, and yes, Motown artists had to abide by certain rules, dress codes, and creative direction. The Monkees, too, were the brainchild of a few TV executives who advertised in *Variety* magazine for "four insane musician boys." The 90s gave birth to boy band impresario Lou Pearlman (Backstreet Boys, 'NSync) and his fail-safe formulas: "one sensitive one," "one dark one," and "one innocent one," etc. What may be different today is the sheer percentage of artists that get "cast" into their fame. As with mooks and midriffs, certain marketing strategies are virtually fail-safe. The concept is best illustrated in the *Brady Bunch* episode known as "Adiós, Johnny Bravo." Hipster talent agents talk Greg into dumping his wholesome family singing act and making a go at a solo career. The formula for his media hype includes a new set of dynamite threads (a tasseled matador suit) and the unsuspecting "Johnny Bravo" getting mobbed by a band of love-crazed teenage girls who were hired to rip his shirt to shreds (the mauling is, of course, captured in publicity photos). Greg soon realizes that his authentic acoustic sound has been unrecognizably doctored with cutting-edge recording technology. "But that's not me!" naïve Greg complains. The agents then confess that Greg was not chosen for his innate talent; he was chosen because he "fit the suit." But righteous Greg will not be duped. "Yeah, I've got a new sound to lay on you," Greg famously declares while ripping up his contract, "the sound of me walkin'."

Today, it seems there is an endless supply of questionably talented stars more than willing to "fit the suit." The market is flooded with teenybopper idols, (a.k.a. pop tarts) who change their facades along with the seasons. In the end, fame may be more about the suit itself than the one who wears it. This drift toward all flash and little substance is evident in the many incidences of stars "caught in the act" of faking. The following cautionary tales were responsible for serious deficits in the "cool capital" of these unlucky performers. Some recovered unscathed; others went down like *Titanic the Musical.*

► **Milli Vanilli:** In 1989 Millie Vanilli was forced to give back their Grammy for lip syncing after their music track jammed and began to skip during a "live" MTV performance. This very public glitch forced many to question the source of the group's talent until finally, the groups creator, Frank Farian, confessed that the Milli Vanilli lead singers didn't sing live—or on their records. As a result of the fall-out, Arista Records dropped the act and deleted the album from its catalogs.[34]

► **Ashlee Simpson:** In 2004 the "dark" younger sister of Jessica blamed her drummer for hitting the wrong button and engaging the "guide track" of the incorrect song while she performed on *Saturday Night Live*. Ashlee danced nervously for a few bars before running off the stage. The larger question, though, became the use of the guide track; why would a performer lip-sync her own voice? The singer then called into *Total Request Live*, attributing her use of a voice track on *SNL* to a bad case of acid reflux. Once again, the public felt duped, and when Ashlee performed off-key (for real) a few months later at the Orange Bowl, the audience booed.[35]

► **Eminem:** A week after the Ashlee debacle, Eminem appeared on *SNL* and, according to many, committed a similar lip-syncing crime. The track was obviously ahead of his lips, and at one point he put the mike down but the vocals kept going. The rapper denied the accusations, admitting only that he *sang along* with a track of his own voice to attain a "double vocal effect."[36]

▶ **Britney Spears:** The lyrics to her massively hyped *MTV Video Music Awards* comeback performance "Gimme More" might not be too difficult to mouth correctly, but Britney appeared to not really give a damn if her mouth moved *at all* while her vocal track blared on.[37] For this, the much-scorned Britney might deserve credit for blatantly exposing the dirty underbelly of pop glitz. Is it possible that Britney's getting tired of her sex-kitten persona? Maybe she's ready to trade in her sequined underwear and high-heeled boots, for a look that's easier on her conscience (as well as her abs). Unlikely, yes, but stranger things have happened.

▶ **Hannah Montana:** Average teen Miley Cyrus plays out her second life onstage as Hannah Montana, the character she portrays on her hit Disney TV series. This pop princess puts on a show with so many head-spinning distractions (dancers, giant video screens, fireworks, moving stages and ramps) that your average adolescent fan is so over-stimulated she *has* to shriek. It was remarkable, then, that anyone at all noticed as the real Hannah hid under a black sheet and disappeared behind a trap door only to be replaced, seconds later, with *another* Hannah. Yes, the Hannah body double stood in as the real Hannah changed costumes, continuing to sing lip-sync as if the original lip-syncing Hannah had never left the stage.[38]

Cross Marketing

The Olsen twins' video series all begin with a relentless assault of product promotions—everything from Mary-Kate and Ashley dolls, book series, and cartoons, all the way to the Mary-Kate and Ashley Fashion and Lifestyle Collections. Lately, just about every rapper, athlete, and pop tart out there has launched his or her own clothing line, sports accessory, and maybe even a kitchen appliance or two. It's as if the star has become the corporation. The corporation, in turn, hopes to reap the cool of the icons it creates.

Create Your Own

CELEBRITY

Choose any combination of the following publicity stunts:

Drive drunk, naked, and blindfolded.

Flash tits.

Partake in weekend marriage/divorce and religious conversion.

Adopt a disabled, third-world child.

Accuse unsuspecting relative of sexual molestation.

Launch little sister pop tart.

Pretend to die.

If gay, become straight.

Bite a cop.

Get banned by Catholic Church.

Shameless Endorsement Hall of Fame

Yes, it's true, Courtney Love really did approve Converse the use of her dead husband's journals. The tortured scrawlings of Kurt Cobain are now immortalized in canvas (high or low top!) as part of Converse's "Century Celebration." Many of course, have deemed Ms. Love's approval as sacrilege. The list below is a collection of similar unholy endorsements, beginning in 1898 with Pope Leo hawking for Vin Mariani's cocaine-infused wine. The pontiff loved turn-of-the-century-Mariani wine so much he carried a personal hipflask to fortify himself in time of need.

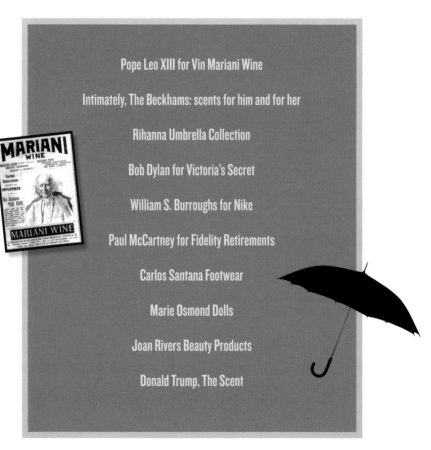

Pope Leo XIII for Vin Mariani Wine

Intimately, The Beckhams: scents for him and for her

Rihanna Umbrella Collection

Bob Dylan for Victoria's Secret

William S. Burroughs for Nike

Paul McCartney for Fidelity Retirements

Carlos Santana Footwear

Marie Osmond Dolls

Joan Rivers Beauty Products

Donald Trump, The Scent

Public Relations to the Rescue!

What happens when big stars get uncooled? Mike Tyson has established a rap sheet which includes a rape conviction, an ear biting, and assaulting various fans and motorists. Yet, each time Mike is released from prison, he celebrates by writing a much-publicized check for some heart-wrenching charitable cause, though his most recent PR stunt (for charity, of course) has caused many to doubt his sincerity: he wants to fight women.[39] Two weeks after Hugh Grant was arrested, pants down, with hooker Devine Brown, Jay Leno famously asked him: "What the hell were you thinking?" Grant's response: "I've never been one, to you know, blow my own trumpet." Other disgraced stars like Mel Gibson impart a three-phase redemption strategy: apologize, go to rehab, and direct a movie about the oppressed Mayan civilization. Self mockery though, this is the new rescue 911 for image emergencies. When Britney Spears's suspected boob job was the laughingstock of every American teenager, what was a girl to do? Go on *Saturday Night Live* and make fun of your boob job! Likewise, when Ashlee Simpson's lip-syncing fiasco nearly sunk her career, she reenacted the *SNL* guffaw for an awards show performance, then seconds later, ribbed her audience, "Only kidding!"[40]

Everything Old Is New Again

> *"Fashion is a form of ugliness so intolerable that we have to alter it every six months."*
>
> ▶ **Oscar Wilde**

Whether it's the empire dress, the mutton-sleeve jacket, or the maxi-, midi-, or miniskirt . . . rest assured, if it's gone away, it's coming back. Those new capris are no different than the culottes your mama wore or the knickers her papa wore. Just as all the great stories have already been told, so have all the great styles already been

The Incarnations of the Modern Straight-leg

1942: Liz Taylor wears calf-hugging **riding pants** in the film *National Velvet*

1965: British Mods plus anorexic socialites like Edie Sedgwick pass out on the couches of Andy Warhol's Factory in **stirrup polyester slacks.**

1956: Audrey Hepburn drags from her cigarette holder wearing narrow **pedal pushers** in *Breakfast at Tiffany's.*

1975: No one but a washed-up housewife is caught dead in those ridiculous pants. **Bell-bottoms** rule the day. Stirrup slacks (now known as the dreaded **stretch pants**) are only sold for five dollars or less in unfashion emporiums like Woolworth's and Kmart.

1997: Pants get big, real big. Baggy is the operative word with styles like **cargo pants** and **parachutes**. Anyone wearing The Melrose or acid-washed leotard jeans is banned from entering New York City nightclubs.

1985: The birth of Spandex inspires Lycra-cotton blends, ultimately spawning the **acid-washed leotard jean.** These pants are often cropped below the knee and stonewashed in various colors like pink and green.

2005: The Gap introduces their new **skinny jeans**, dubbing them The Audrey. Advertising campaign uses Audrey Hepburn movie clips.

1992: Tori Spelling breaks out The Melrose, **uber-high-waisted jeans** so narrow at the ankle that the heels had to be wedged free with a shoe horn.

2001: Inspired by 60s Mods and Emo Indy rockers like The Strokes, kids mull around alternative coffee shops in low-riding **drainpipes**.

exhausted . . . until they are pulled out of the fashion-don't bag, fumigated, and renamed.

The Fashion Police

"Beware of all enterprises which require new clothes."

▶ **Henry David Thoreau**

We all know about the fashion police, and maybe we even glance twice at those fashion-page "don'ts" to see if maybe, just maybe, the stealthy photographer caught one of us sitting at that bus stop unaware. Did we dare to leave the house with back cleavage, exposed knee-highs, or another sad case of undersized back pockets? Well, the fashion police have been around much longer than *Glamour* magazine. Roman Emperor Honorius put forth a decree that prohibited men from wearing such styles as the crude and vulgar trousers. Roman prostitutes were assigned flame-colored togas, and later, striped cloaks (one way to stand out in a crowd); they were also required to dye their hair blonde. Medieval sumptuary laws were enacted to regulate morally extravagant forms of dress. The government saw fit to curb conspicuous consumption; therefore, only a select noble class was granted permission to wear preferred silks and other luxurious fabrics.[41] Those dressing beyond their means were prosecuted—all this to protect the vulnerable souls of the naïve lower classes. And of course, many Middle Eastern cultures today still prohibit women from all but the most conservative styles of dress.

What we wear says everything about our social class. While it may be considered bad taste for the 7-Eleven clerk down the street to dress like Paris Hilton, she can no longer be arrested for it. Paradoxically, it may be more common today to see people from the upper classes dressing "down," wearing such fashion marvels as the white suburban doo rag. This may be attributed to the more modern phenomenon of marketing "the cool mystique," as opposed to simply promoting your run-of-the-mill prestige.

The Baggy Pants Story

It is widely believed that gang members outside of prison stopped wearing their belts as a sign of allegiance to their brethren inside the prisons, whose belts were confiscated to prevent hangings. Others contend that the trend was begun by shoplifters in the 1980s to conceal merchandise as large as sneakers. The falling-down crotch is often parallel with the wearer's knees, exposing a pair of low-riding boxer shorts. The standard visible ass-crack even inspired one Virginia delegate to champion "The Droopy Drawers Bill." "It's called underwear for a reason!" claimed John Reid.[42] The unpassed bill, which called for fining all cracks, thongs, and boxers, was parodied on many talk shows. The controversial pants are also a big hit on YouTube with a plethora of security videos featuring botched robbery runaways due to the crippling "droop factor."

It didn't take long for Madison Avenue to tap black style's potential. Baggy pants became enormously popular with white affluent teenagers. This is why white kids from Paramus, New Jersey, pay big money to dress like incarcerated gangsters and why pimp costumes from

iParty (grills included) were number-one bestsellers for white teenage boys on Halloween. Wiggers, wangsters, and wegros are only a few of the terms used to describe this brazen adaptation of black style by white kids. Writer Donnell Alexander, in an article for *Might Magazine*, describes the disconnect like this:

> *"There's a gang of cool white folks, all of whom exist that way because they've found their essential selves amid the abundant and ultimately numbing media replications of the coolness vibe and the richness of real life. And there's a whole slew more of them ready to sign up if you tell 'em where. But your average wigger in the rap section of Sam Goody ain't gone nowhere; she or he hasn't necessarily learned shit about the depth and breadth of cool, about making a dollar out of 15 cents."*[43]

Killer Fashion: So Cool It Hurts

"What a deformed thief this fashion is."
▶ **William Shakespeare,** *Much Ado About Nothing*

Perhaps nothing illustrates the power of cool better than a participant's willingness, at any cost, to subscribe to a particular fashion. The following styles were so cool they hurt, really hurt. Despite their commercial success, these fads limited their victims in some significant physical way, occasionally resulting in death. It may be hard for women today to imagine beauty defined as a twelve-inch corseted waist, that is, until they tune into a procedure or two on *Extreme Makeover*. What is cool in one fashion era may appear barbaric to the next; yet, throughout fashion history, this legacy of painful extremes has prevailed.

▶ **Whalebone corsets:** In 1860 there were nearly 4,000 corsetières working in Paris. In England at least 35,000 people were employed in the burgeoning industry, mostly female. By 1880, Germany alone was exporting over 600,000 corsets annually to America.[44] It's obvious then, why the corset lobby wanted to keep women in shape. These extreme under-wonders might have looked good on the fainting couch, but they've been associated with a slew of medical conditions such as deep vein thrombosis, rib deformation, scoliosis, respiratory complications, and prolapsed uteri, to name a few. Victorian girls began "training" as adolescents, hoping to attain the ideal 12-inch "wasp waist" as they approached marriageable age. Despite suffrage and the feminist revolution, corsets are back again today. Now called body shapers, these "comfortable" high tech body suits promise to shrink women down by at least one dress size.

▶ **The Lotus Shoe:** Beginning in 10th century China, the practice of foot binding would last all the way up to the twentieth century. Small feet, a symbol of beauty and submission, were a way to ensure a woman's economic security. The smaller the feet, the more marriageable she was. Bound feet also signaled financial success because it implied that a husband could afford to keep a wife incapable of physical labor. Beginning at age six, girls' feet were

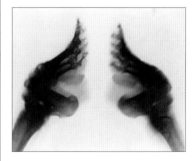

wrapped in bandages to prevent normal development. The ideal length was three to six inches. Of course, the custom rendered women immobile, resulting often in deadly infections and muscular atrophy.

▶ **Jimmy Choo Dagger-Toe Shoe:** *Sex in the City*'s Carrie had a penchant for $600 Jimmy Choo shoes. Some blame this for the recent spate of foot surgeries to get into a pair of dagger-toe shoes, which even according to Jimmy himself, don't look good on women with big feet. One New York surgery center, the Institute Beaute, charges $2,500 to shorten each toe and $500 per collagen injection to restore lost padding to the ball of the high-heeled foot. As Choo stilettos flew off the shelves (their sales increased exponentially once Carrie slipped them on) *The Wall Street Journal* reported a huge boom in podiatry products such as toe tonics, blister bandages and special high heel inserts.[45]

▶ **Baggy Pants:** These pants raked in millions for the apparel industry, yet the style does have its limitations. The knee-level crotch has been known to cause more than a few complications. The style has even been deemed dangerous by gang members who leave them home on fight nights. Baggy pants and crime are never a wise combination. Cops are all too happy to tackle suspects to the ground, but it makes the job a whole lot easier when the suspect's pants take him down first. In one case, a suspect went down when his wide legs snagged on a fence post. The "wide ones" were even blamed for the murder of Kendraya Glasper. The accused, Vincent Cornelius, claimed he accidentally fired his .357-caliber revolver twice as he stood outside a car in which Glasper was sitting. The reason? Slippage. Cornelius contended that when his pants slipped, he mistakenly pulled the gun out of his pocket, then hit his arm against the side of the car, causing it to fire. The sound startled him, he said, resulting in the second shot.[46]

▶ **The Farrah Fawcett Tan**: Nowadays the beaches are rife with kids smothered in pasty white sun block. (Roll them in sand for that cinnamon donut effect!) Long before blue, spray-on, waterproof, SPF 1,000 there was oil—oil that sizzled and melted into your red, inflaming skin. Toasted beach beauties like Bo Derek and Farrah Fawcett made white girls want to be brown, and this often required shedding six dead layers of lizard skin first. All over America, teenage girls basted in sweet-smelling oils with reflectors (usually a *Dark Side of the Moon* album covered in tin foil) held under their chins. Tanning industry giants like Coppertone and *Bain De Soleil* were raking in millions. Meanwhile there was a hole in the ozone layer the size of Africa. Little did the peeling ones know that their incidence of skin cancer would increase by at least 75%.

▶ **Breast Implants:** Body augmentation has far surpassed the corset in terms of fiscal success. This lucrative industry has increased 700% since 1992. Last year, in the United States alone, over ten billion dollars was spent on cosmetic surgery. In the early 1900s, before saline or silicone breast implants, various other substances were experimented with, often with deadly results. These included ox cartilage, foam sponges, and ground rubber.[47] During World War II, Japanese prostitutes began using silicone breast injections to lure American GIs and by the early Sixties an estimated 50,000 women had received them. These shots often caused granulomas and tissue-hardening so severe that mastectomies were required for treatment. Saline and silicone-filled breast implants were introduced in the mid-Sixties and remain the most popular materials for breast augmentation today. While many studies have touted their relative safety, conditions such as ruptures, leaking, capsular contracture, implant extrusion, tissue necrosis, and various systemic diseases have been reported by implant patients.[48] Gone are the days when flat-chested girls secretly ordered breast enhancement creams from the back of magazines. "Mom, Dad, can I get boobs and a car for graduation?" An estimated 9,000 girls under the age of twenty underwent breast enhancement surgery last year and that number is dramatically on the rise.[49]

▶ **Belladonna Eyes:** This deadly nightshade plant contains the chemical atropine, which Victorian women would drop into their eyes to dilate their pupils. This, according to the fashion of the day, made their eyes luminescent and romantically irresistible. It also made them hallucinate, blind, and sometimes even die.[50] The plant's name was derived from this intended usage as *Belladonna* translates to "Beautiful Lady." (Of course, women often lost their allure when they started complaining of imaginary snakes and melting walls.)

▶ **Dead White:** When the Countess of Coventry died in 1760, the newspapers claimed she was a "victim of cosmetics." While the pale look was popular in Roman times, it reached its zenith in the 1800s. Both men and women painted their faces with a mixture of vinegar and white lead. Apparently, the concoction caused a vicious cycle of irritation and scarring which then needed to be covered up with *even more* whitening solutions. By 1869 the American Medical Association linked certain cosmetic products to lead palsy with symptoms including nausea, headaches, muscle atrophy, and even paralysis.[51]

Another deadly powder was known as widow powder. "Aqua Toffana" was the brainchild of cosmetics maven Giulia Toffana, her preferred clients being the unhappy wives of wealthy husbands. This face powder was all the rage back in Renaissance Italy; it contained arsenic, lead, and possibly belladonna. Giulia herself instructed her clients in the use of her product: it could be applied to the woman's cheeks before hello and goodbye pecks, or simply diluted into the husband's food and wine. In other words, the poisoning could take place "accidentally" or intentionally. Ultimately, the secrets of Aqua Toffana were revealed, but not before the alleged deaths of 600 people. In 1659 Giulia was executed in Rome.[52]

▶ **The Lip:** Actors and actresses alike have gotten "the lip." Watching movies today, one comes to wonder if every face onscreen isn't interrelated—say from the same Celtic tribe of pouty-lipped Gauls. No, it's just the filler. Sometimes the implants are synthetic, like Gore-Tex or UltraSoft. Other fillers are made of human cadaveric tissue (yes, from *corpses!*) Lips gone wrong can lead to such complications as extrusion, migration, permanent bruising, scar tissue, HIV transmission, and infection. Pop singer Pete Burns (of Dead or Alive) is suing his plastic surgeon, claiming his lip job looked like he had been "mutilated with a Stanley knife."[53] The greatest hazard of all, though, may be unknowingly looking like a trout. A few of the accused may be: Cher, Meg Ryan, Jocelyn Wildenstein, Mickey Rourke.

Cool Check

Don't believe the hype? You're not alone. After all, the hype is like that all-too-eager friend who's in your face every time you turn around. Today, hip advertisers want to replace parents as authority figures, yet they also want to be the bestest pal, the one who really gets that misunderstood teen. This, as any real parent can tell you, is a Catch-22. And kids, for the most part, see through it. They are beginning to resent the media's pursuit of their culture. This is the irony of coolhunting: whatever it catches, it kills. So rather than being agents of cool, the advertiser is more like the grim reaper of cool. It's no wonder so many artists have turned to the power of independent forums such as YouTube, Facebook, and MySpace. Douglas Rushkoff, in the PBS documentary "The Merchants of Cool" refers to the feedback loop like this:

> *"The media watches kids and then sells them an image of themselves. Then kids watch those images and aspire to be what they see in the TV set. And the media is there watching them do that in order to craft new images for them, and so on."*[54]

And when kids understandably rebel against the mainstream with movements like punk and rage rock, that too gets sucked up by the machine and sold back to them. In the end, of course, authentic cool cannot be hunted down or conjured up, nor can it be packaged and sold.

As a backlash against this media onslaught, the obvious has officially come to be: *It's cool to be uncool.* Websites like Theuncoolhunter.com and Satchelofgravel.com leave the definition of cool up to you. These democratic forums, unlike MTV, operate beyond the art directors, hucksters, and feedback loops.

The uncoolhunter's manifesto is this:

"*Someone asked the Dalai Lama, 'What is fashion?' and he answered: 'What is out of fashion.' Taking into account this postulate, a group of observers intend to glimpse a vanguard in the anti-global non-trends. Our goal is to observe everyday life and point out the uncool circuits, the anti-hegemonic culture. From an objective and sharp look at the non-trends, we want to make the 'off culture' known because it is left aside by what seems to be emergent.*"[55]

Uncoolhunter.com even sponsors an uncool art show each year in Buenos Aires. Everyone is invited to post on their site with "information related to the kitsch, the bizarre, the freak, the surreal, the hyper-real, the sub-professional, or everything that does not fit in the cool or elite culture." Other anti-hype sites like Satchel of Gravel and Ad Busters offer critiques (often hilarious) on the waste and absurdities of consumer culture.

Outsider Cool

Often, an uneasy dynamic exists between the eccentric and the downright unmarketable. The trick may be knowing which is which. Controversial art is risky to market but often worth the effort. Yet to be truly authentic a rebellion must be commercial-free. Imagine, "The Revolution (brought to you by . . . .)" The more objectionable the art, the more likely it is to be commercially perused. Bands like the indigestible Sex Pistols formed as an answer to "increasingly safe and bloated progressive rock." They goaded the record industry to "Market this, I dare you." Well, EMI was the first to try, but this company soon dumped them as the band's public-relations disasters began to mount. "I don't understand it," member Johnny Rotten replied, "All we were trying to do is destroy everything." Similar tales of packaged rebellion abound in the record industry with The Beastie Boys, Eminem, Insane Clown Posse, Marilyn Manson, and 50 Cent, to name a few. Outsider cool, on the other hand, is nearly unexploitable. The following cultural oddities, (at least for the time being) are just too damn weird to market.

▶ **Tommy the Clown:** Tommy Johnson's clown persona was created in response to the bling excesses of mainstream Hip Hop. His act, an amalgam of magic, games, and dance, was originally developed for kids' birthday parties. He soon opened Tommy the Clown's Hip Hop Academy of Dance and is now known as the father of krumpin' (a dance style that mixes face painting, wrestling, kung fu, circus, and break dancing). Tommy and his kids have performed all over the world. Not bad for a birthday party clown.[56]

▶ **Nude Air Travel:** Castaways Travel has been a leader in the clothing-optional tour industry since 1984, yet it wasn't until May of 2003 that it offered the first-ever nude flight from Miami to Cancun.[57] (Ass towels provided free of charge.)

▶ **Subway Parties:** These celebrations occur, most often, on the last car of the train. They tend to include music, costumes, and the sprinkling of glitter. One goal is to spread mirth among the curmudgeonly masses; another is to have fun and freak commuters out. The partiers view subway travel as an art form rather than simply another circle of hell. At times the parties have themes like a color, Dr. Seuss, or "no pants."[58]

▶ **Wife Carrying**: This sport supposedly originated in Sonkajarvi Finland where a Viking chose his woman mate by running into her village, hoisting her over his shoulders and carrying her away. Wife-carrying competitions take place in Maine, Michigan, Wisconsin, and Finland. The winners often receive their wife's weight in beer.[59]

▶ **Bathtub Racing:** Over land and over sea, beware of speeding porcelain bathtubs. Souped-up any number of creative ways, (wheels, motors, sails) these tubs can speed, and do. Nanaimo Canada (otherwise know as Tub City) is home to the largest annual tub-racing competition.[60]

▶ **Crying Clubs:** Apparently, this trend began in Tokyo as an outlet for stressed-out Japanese businessmen. The practice of intentional crying is a physiologist-approved method of emotional cleansing. The stressed were encouraged to rent (by the hour) specialized hotel rooms which played crying movies. Or if businessmen preferred to weep with others, they could attend a group cry-a-thon. The trend soon traveled to England with the opening of "Loss," a new nightclub, which bills itself as "an evening of misery." With or without the help of onions, clubbers come to indulge themselves in the act of weeping.[61] Yet another manifestation of PDC (Public Displays of Crying) can be found on crying-whileeating.com. Users of this forum are invited to post short QuickTime videos of themselves crying with a caption describing the meal being consumed as well as the root of their distress (global warming, bad break-up, no cable, etc).

Big daddy of crumpin'

Crying clubber

The Business of Cool: Conclusion

Madison Avenue, at best, packages and sells back inauthentic imitations of cool, blips they captured in the fringe and try to keep alive long enough to market. Though, just like the lightening bug, that blip is often dead by the time the lid comes off the jar. At worst, the media attempt to create their own sensations from scratch, and these, like Johnny Bravo, are often the most transparent of all. Another popular option, marketing genuine rebels—while rabidly profitable—is always fraught with peril. While signed with A&M Records, Sex Pistol Sid Vicious wrecked the managing director's office and threw up on his desk; A&M dumped the band accordingly.[62] At this point, one might assume that the band had fulfilled its original prophecy: they were the unmarketable anti-Beatles; yet this didn't deter Virgin Records from giving them one last try. Eight months later, at the band's final performance, Johnny Rotten asked the audience "Ever get the feeling you've been cheated?"[63] Then he threw the microphone down and exited the stage. Unlike the mounting list of aging rockers who have traded in their cool for fat commercial payoffs, the Sex Pistols have continued to make a career out of loathing The Man. Recently, the band was inducted into the Rock and Roll Hall of Fame, yet the remaining members called the museum a "piss stain" and refused to attend the ceremony.[64]

Cool, like beauty, is in the eye of the beholder. Plastic surgery, crippling fashions, and deadly habits like smoking are only a few of the extremes people are willing to submit to, all for the sake of style. Fashion is cyclical, even predictable, but cool exists outside the repetitive tides of style in/style out. Classic cool may eventually land inside the mainstream, but it never begins there. Conversely, outsider cool rarely sets foot in the middle-of-the-road. Outsider cool is where human eccentricities thrive and breed—a loving home for every freakazoid, oddball, and nut job who did as they damn well pleased. And if that corporation knocks on their door despite their raving weirdness, outsider cool resists. Johnny Rotten's response to the Hall of Fame invite included sentiments such as these: "We're not your monkeys . . . You're not paying attention... Outside this shit-stem is the real SEX PISTOL."[65] Unfortunately, the *real* Sex Pistol appeared as a C-list star on the reality show *I'm a Celebrity—Get Me Out of Here!* Rotten did, however, manage to call the show's viewers "fucking cunts" on live TV.[66] And reality TV has certainly earned its disdain—so why not *at least try* to package the anti-reality TV revolution? Former Sex Pistols manager Malcolm McLaren's next rumored venture is supposedly in the works: the anti-Pop Idol. His goal: to knock idol talent shows "off the altar." In this proposed stab at idol mania, viewers would be asked to choose the worst, not the best. "One lesson," McLaren explains, "is making the worthless valuable, then making ugliness beautiful."[67] And here, the feedback loop begins again.

Johnny Rotten

Cool

Part 4

THE COOLHUNTER'S
FIELD GUIDE

The Coolhunter's Field Guide: Introduction

This section will attempt to classify particular phylums of cool in the cultural landscape just as Darwin—heading for the Galapagos Islands—set out to decode life
as he knew it. Decoding cool, in fact, may be as fraught with controversy as
Darwin's *Origin of Species*. Research and travel weren't easy on Charles, a lifelong
hypochondriac plagued with ulcers, boils, tremors, and heart palpitations. His work
was received like the bubonic plague, a point to keep in mind as the reader browses
through the following subdivisions. No doubt, the assertive will find omissions in
the examples to follow as well as names that might be challenged under the heading: "More of the Famous." For this reason, apologies are offered in advance. Feel
free to grab that thick black permanent marker and black out or add in any offend-
ing or omitted persons you feel strongly about. Cool, after all, is in the eye of the
beholder.

Under the heading "Often Mimicked By" the social observer is offered various tips on exposing the many imposters of cool. Just as the poison dart frog (tox-
icity being the ultimate evolutionary advantage) is imitated by any number of
non-poisonous "mimic species," the authentically cool are imitated by a plethora
of social opportunists—Elvis impersonators are only the tip of this iceberg. For
example, the cool type "Hard Luck Cool" is often impersonated by authors in the

form of fabricated memoirs—writers simply inventing the dysfunctional childhoods they never had. So, the next time you're out on an impromptu coolhunting expedition, maybe lounging on a park bench, edging up to that dance floor, or braving the renewal line at the DMV—see if you don't just observe a few of the following classic cool types.

The Cool Teacher

It is often hard to differentiate between the Cool Teacher and the teacher who wanted to be cool way back in junior high but wasn't. The list of famous Cool Teachers is virtually non-existent as truly cool teachers are humble and rarely achieve celebrity status. The only way this cool type becomes famous is via fiction when a Lifetime-style movie is made about the humble one's understated greatness. Occasionally, the phrase "based on a true story" is momentarily flashed onto the screen, yet more often than not, the actual Cool Teacher remains anonymous. Scenes abound with the Cool Teacher struggling with The Man over his or her unconventional teaching methods, which may include madcap outdoor instruction and impromptu field trips to the seedier parts of town. Frequently, the job of the Cool Teacher is threatened, either by budget cuts, or a meathead principal who fails to perceive his or her brilliance.

The true Cool Teacher is the one students follow around like a deity. Rarely does this fabulously popular teacher have to summon discipline by dropping large books flat onto the floor because students are too engaged to misbehave. Occasionally, a student may rise to challenge the Cool Teacher to a battle of wits. These situations always turn out badly for the challenger, as the Cool Teacher is never humiliated by the threatening upstart. The wise-ass student is handily subdued, often to the raucous laughter of classmates, and the beloved teacher, once again, prevails. Cool Teachers are often full of hidden talents. They may, for example attend a student bar mitzvah and bust into a fit of unexpected moonwalking on the dance floor. Or, at the school band concert, the Cool Teacher may suddenly grab a pair of drumsticks and lay down a five-minute, mind-blowing drum solo. These blackboard heroes generally care little about traditional notions of cool and may therefore wear unfashionable, ill-fitting clothes. Not surprisingly, this merely adds to their mystique.

More of the Famous

Fictitious: Mr. "S" (Jack Black) in *School of Rock*, Mr. Keating (Robin Williams) in *Dead Poet's Society*, Ms. Johnson (Michelle Pfeiffer) in *Dangerous Minds*, Mr. Holland (Richard Dreyfuss) in *Mr. Holland's Opus*, Ms. Guaspari (Meryl Streep) in *Music of the Heart*, Mr. Thackeray (Sidney Poitier) in *To Sir With Love*, Mr. Chips in *Goodbye, Mr. Chips*

Habitat

Classrooms (particularly underprivileged), sports fields, hovel apartments, shit-box cars.

Often Mimicked By

Pedophiles, aimless slackers, interloping substitutes, and creepy coaches. These mimics may casually swear in the classroom, therefore inciting an unexpected tidal wave of adolescent profanity. Too-hip teachers who are lax with discipline might soon find themselves surrounded by adolescent savages wielding slingshot rulers loaded with thumbtacks. These imposters often respond to a student's commentary with "Cool," rather than, "Excellent observation Johnny." They may nonchalantly drop hints about their alternative lifestyle by leaving massive nightclub stamps on their hands. Their bike helmets may be plastered with inflammatory stickers. Also notice-able may be packs of poorly concealed rolling papers. References to obscure YouTube videos or Facebook phenomenon are often dropped to signal the mimic's ageless affinity for the fly and dope. They might overtly flirt with students in hopes of generating the forbidden sexual tension which Sting made famous in his cautionary ballad, "Don't Stand So Close to Me."

Rebel Cool

The most shining example of Rebel Cool might be the famous "Unknown Rebel" of the 1989 Tiananmen Square uprisings. Shortly after the Chinese government lashed out, killing hundreds of demonstrators, this geekish everyday man, apparently on his way home from shopping, decided to run out into the middle of the Avenue of Eternal Peace and intercept a convoy of seventeen approaching tanks. With shopping bags in hand, the Unknown Rebel stood face to face with the massive leading tank, stopping it in its tracks. Many agree that there were two heroes that day, The Unknown Rebel and the

Unknown Soldier who refused to run him down.[1] The Unknown Rebel represents all the anonymous nobodies who ever fought The Man—particularly those who fought The Man and lost. Typically, public record favors the dynamic, good-looking rebels like Che Guevara who were martyred in their prime. But all those not-so-hot rebels must be acknowledged too—particularly those who committed their lives to a seemingly impossible cause. Susan B. Anthony devoted most of her 86 years to securing the vote for women. This childless bachelorette died fourteen years before the Nineteenth Amendment was ratified, and the only recognition she ever got was her dower face on a 1979 dollar coin, which was so often mistaken for a quarter that many rallied for the damn thing to be taken out of circulation. But Susan B. didn't do it for the money.

Susan B. Anthony: She didn't do it for the money.

Cool Rebels are known for acts of defiance, which may be second nature to them, yet appear wildly courageous to the rest of us. When a judge ordered Miss Anthony to pay a hundred dollar fine for voting, she replied, "May it please your honor, I will never pay a dollar of your unjust penalty."[2] And, she never *did* pay that fine. Rebel Cool is the steadfast determination of Margaret Sanger, who rowed a boat out into the East River in the middle of the night to retrieve floating boxes of contraband French diaphragms so American women could get pregnant only if they *wanted* to. Or, imagine Martin Luther, nailing his 95 Theses to the door of Castle Church, sweat rolling down his infuriated face. Now *there's* a way to question church authority. Luther fig-

Margaret Sanger: diaphragm smuggler

ured, hey, why not come right out and ask the Pope what's up with the sale of indul-gences and by the way, "Why build the Basilica of Saint Peter with the money of poor believers rather than the Pope's own money?"[3] His nailed-up grievances were so per-tinent, in fact, that they became the basis of the Protestant Reformation.

One of the most famous acts of artistic defiance belongs to Cool Rebel Diego Rivera in the story of the Lenin head. Rivera, a known Communist sympathizer, was hired by Nelson Rockefeller to paint a mural in New York's Rockefeller Center. In it, Rivera slipped in a portrait of Vladimir Lenin, which Nelson spotted and demanded he remove. Rivera refused, so Rockefeller had the mural reduced to dust.[4] As a result, Rivera's escalating U.S. mural career summarily ended, though he did end up with one great cocktail-party story. In honor of Rivera, the act of the artist sticking it to the patron is sometimes referred to as "pulling a Leninhead."

The do-gooder exhibits the most altruistic manifestation of Rebel Cool. Do-gooder rebels often possess the missionary zeal of Jesus, Gandhi, and Martin Luther King. The do-gooder's cause is often more legitimately humanitarian than the unshaven guerilla rebel who tends to sleep outdoors. The do-gooder rebel is all big-picture—motivating the masses and executing a "master plan." Sometimes the do-gooder's actions exact watershed cultural changes; other times decades of sacrifice and perseverance result in little change at all. In fact, today's activists, in the face of such issues as global warming, may feel like Sisyphus rolling his big rock uphill for all of eternity. To the befuddled contemporary activist, Andrew Boyd (head of Billionaires for Bush) offers the following advice in his book *Daily Afflictions*:

> "Do you dedicate yourself to an impossible cause? Or do you look after your own, making do as best you can. The choice is clear; you must dedicate yourself to an impossible cause. Why? Because we are all incurable. Because solidarity is a form of tenderness. Because the simple act of caring for the world is itself a victory. Take a stand—not because it will lead to anything but because it is the right thing to do."[5]

Following in the footsteps of the old prankster rebels like Abbie Hoffman and Jerry Rubin, Andrew Boyd's modern-day crusade takes the form of street theater. For example, his Billionaires for Bush campaign mobilized hordes of activists (dressed in diamonds, furs, and tails) to march down to G.O.P. headquarters with a gigantic check made out for "Whatever It Takes."

Unlike Marlon Brando in *The Wild Ones*, most Cool Rebels don't even own a leather jacket or a motorcycle to pose on. They may dress in the green army fatigues of Castro, the unraveling sombrero of Emiliano Zapata, or the prison uniform of Nelson Mandela. Cool Rebels don't wear famous fashions, they make fashions famous: Che Guevara's black beret, Alice Paul's purple hat, even the Quaker bonnet of *The Woman's Bible* author Elizabeth Cady Stanton.

What makes a rebel authentic is this: unwavering devotion to a just cause. For example, self-serving crime is not a just cause—revolution against an oppressive power is. Frequently these dissenters must pay a price for their brazen behavior. Sometimes that price is merely egg on the face, other times the rebels are alienated by their beloved church or scientific community. And of course, there is always the ultimate sacrifice—when the rebel is called to join the ranks of martyrs.

More of the Famous

Actual: Joan of Arc, Galileo, Jackie Robinson, John Lennon, Leon Trotsky, Cesar Chavez, Rosa Parks, Mother

Billionaires for Bush

Joan of Arc

Teresa. *Fictitious:* Robin Hood, Norma Rae (Sally Fields), Luke Skywalker (Mark Hamill) in *Star Wars*.

Habitat

Guerilla hideouts, unheated basements, political rallies, revolutionary uprisings, jails, factory break rooms.

Often Mimicked By

Rebels without a cause and criminal meanies like Machine Gun Kelly motivated not by altruism, but by greed and revenge. Rebels without a cause may take the form of pouty-faced youth with furrowed brows. They may look attractive in their messy hair and leather jackets, though the alienated-delinquent act goes quickly stale. In *Rebel Without a Cause*, James Dean is a brooding teen stifled by repressed 1950s values. Yes, we feel for him, but we may also want to slap him around and see him get a job as, say, a White Castle burger boy. The film did capture the angst of America's post-war youth. Unfortunately, Dean died in a car accident a month before the movie opened. He never got to do what so many disillusioned American youth of the day did: hitchhike to California, drop acid, question authority, and then . . . become a White Castle burger boy or some other humbling equivalent. (Giveaways may include: intentional unemployment, risk-taking behaviors such as racing stolen cars towards cliff edges, exposed weaponry, and parents that just don't understand.)

Quirkster Cool

At first, these pioneers are nearly laughed off the stage. If the status quo is front and center, these guys thrive in outer orbit. At least part of what makes them so endearing is their outright indifference to the standard cool *du jour*, as if they were born to break molds without even trying. Most Cool Quirksters live their strange lives outside the limelight, famous only in small circles that may claim these eccentrics as their very own ambassadors to the "other side." Occasionally, when the quirky ones *do* stumble upon immense success, it's as if their fame were the result of some freak accident. Take the case of Jeanine Deckers, a cloistered nun in a remote Belgian convent. Encouraged by her fellow Sisters to record an album, the Singing Nun ended up with a number one single, a gig on *The Ed Sullivan Show*, and a Hollywood movie. Yet another habit-sporting maverick would be Sister Wendy, the PBS pop sensation with her charming buck-toothed smile. This hermitic nun decided, at the age of sixty, to pursue her passion for art history. While her video museum tours made their own art history, Sister Wendy continued to live in her tiny trailer on the grounds of her Carmelite monastery. Her humble disposition, combined with her unbridled enthusiasm for art, has even inspired the hip West End musical, *Postcards from God*.

Sister Wendy: PBS pop sensation

Many who are drawn to the Quirkster Cool archetype tend to be artistic by nature. So driven by their creative passions, these oddballs often stumble around in the concrete world unprepared—as if their civilian clothes were merely costumes for some mandatory play. The real world, after all, may be all that stands between the quirky and their muses. Alexander Calder, for example, created his own tiny kinetic circus out of wire, cloth, and various found objects. The entire circus fit into a few suitcases which he would carry along to avant-garde parties, set up, and act out, with different voices for each

Andy Warhol appeared on The Love Boat.

Truman Capote

moveable character. His performances created such a *fureur* in Paris that Calder began to collect admission fees to help pay his rent.[6] In similar crackpot style, Salvador Dalí appeared on *The Tonight Show* and refused to sit in an actual chair, preferring instead the leather rhinoceros that he brought along with him.[7]

While some Quirkster Cools shied away from the public eye, others like Andy Warhol and Truman Capote thrived in the glare of celebrity. The anointed king of hipster culture and the New York underground, Warhol made quirk an art form unto itself. While his legendary Factory was the playground of the beautiful, strung-out, and self-proclaimed hip, Andy created his own criteria of cool. When Lou Reed's set was over for the night, and little Edie Sedgwick, passed out on the sofa, was covered with a blanket, Andy left The Factory and went home to the Upper East Side apartment he shared with his sweet old mother, who lived there with him for nearly twenty years. Andy also went to church nearly every day and—cool be damned—he even made an appearance on *The Love Boat*.[8] And of course, there was Truman Capote, often referred to as high society's "strangest little man" who was known for orchestrating his grandiose "Black and White" balls. Why? So *he* could be seen. At the opposite end of the spectrum was obsessive sculptor Joseph Cornell who rarely left the cluttered basement of the modest home he shared with his invalid brother and domineering mother.

More of the Famous

Actual: Vincent Van Gogh, Emily Dickinson, the Marx Brothers, Charlie Chaplin, Sun Ra, Antoni Gaudi, The Smothers Brothers, Erik Satie, Tim Burton, Howie Mandel. *Fictitious:* Ignatius J. Reilly from *Confederacy of Dunces*, Amelie (Audrey Tautou), Max Fisher (Jason Schwartzman) in *Rushmore.*

Habitat

Unheated studio apartments, art happenings, small trailers, open-mic nights, convents, circus rings.

Often Mimicked By

The criminally insane, innocuous whackos, and artsy slackers. At times, the line between out-and-out nut job and Quirkster Cool may be difficult to determine. Indeed, the quirky tend to frolic in the nether regions of socially acceptable behavior. A cutting-edge performance may be no more than one degree away from an "acting out" mental patient. One question the observer may want to ask is: "Am I present as a hostage or being entertained on my own free will?" If the performer is truly Quirkster Cool, this question rarely comes to mind. The two most common imposters of Quirkster Cools tend to exist at either end of the weirdo spectrum. The first being people who may be all too eager to tell you *just how weird they are.* These bogus jesters may wear "wacky" hats that include foam antlers or T-shirts with ironic messages, even the highly controversial "Utilikilt." They may exhibit conversation-stopping behaviors such as the operatic party outburst, or suddenly drop to the floor and contort their bodies in any number of strange positions. Do not confuse these unwieldy fools with true Quirkster Cools. Likewise, there is an obvious difference between the brilliantly eccentric and the dangerously unmedicated. The latter may deliver rapid-fire street sermons with spittle-flying passion. These fervent lectures may at first sound enticing, until you notice that ankle monitor. The lack of matching shoes or a bungee cord belt buckle should not be interpreted as some kind of style proclamation, but rather the result of living on the lam.

Josephine Baker

Mother Jones

Cool Mom

She's the one that the *other* moms whisper about—the playground loner content to sit on the "far bench" immersed in her tattered copy of *Zen and the Art of Motorcycle Maintenance*. The Cool Mom is without pretense, freely admitting her desire to murder her misbehaving child. "What," she might snap back at the righteously appalled, "like *you've* never thought about it?" Cool Moms never partake in boogeyman hearsay about razor blades in apples, toddler abductions, or strychnine poisoning—they may, in fact, wipe the dirt off of their kid's dropped donut and hand it right back to them. These moms are not bothered by their outsider status and secretly enjoy their ability to shock the wholesome/nurturer moms with their foul mouths and alternative clothes. Unlike the scores of asexual moms who may have renounced their career aspirations along with their senses of humor, the Cool Mom is often wry, sexy and still determined to achieve *something* despite the demands of motherhood. To keep their mojos up and running, Cool Moms may flirt unabashedly with coffee baristas, take up the unicycle, or frequent karaoke bars.

The Cool Mom's children, encouraged to dress themselves, are known for their tendency to attend school in costumes such as dishtowel capes, tutus, and Samurai pillowcases. The gender of the cool one's offspring is frequently ambiguous due to androgynous or gender-reversing clothing and hairstyles. Cool Moms are also known for their own gender-bending talents; for example, an affinity for welding and power tools. Broken Tonka Truck? Bad stroller wheel? No problem, Cool Mom is on it with her blowtorch.

More of the Famous

Actual: Mother Jones, Josephine Baker, Rosie O'Donnell. *Fictitious:* Sarah (Samantha Morton) from *In America*, Lorelai Gilmore (Lauren Graham) from *The Gilmore Girls*, Adele August (Susan Sarandon), in *Anywhere But Here*, Diane Freeling (Jobeth Williams) in *Poltergeist.*

Habitat

Seedier urban playgrounds, grammar-school hallways, karaoke bars, adult education plumbing classes, thrift shops.

Often Mimicked By

Moms with icky hickeys, creepy boyfriends, and visible tattoos. The dangers here are best defined by Holly Hunter's character, Melanie, in the movie *Thirteen*. This mom dressed primarily in hot little ensembles off the Juniors' racks and looked better in her skintight jeans that her thirteen-year-old daughter. All the daughter's friends, of course, thought the Holly Hunter mom was the coolest mom in town, and this Cool Mom was summoned daily for rides, money, and crash pad privileges. It was not long, of course, before this Too Cool Mom was running an impromptu home psych hospital for kleptomaniac, drug-addicted, sex-crazed teenage girls. A distinction must always be made between the doormat mom and the Cool Mom who is never uncomfortable asserting her authority. Things can get ugly when that pot-smoking mom refuses to buy the keg for the 8th-grade graduation party. And what if mom *does* cave in and buy the keg? Is her cashing in for hero billing really worth all the teenage vomit such a decision guarantees? The Too Cool Mom is often trying to work out her own tumultuous adolescence—this time as Chrissy Hynde. She'll never be just another *one of the kids,* though, because of her obvious access to any number of grown up goodies: legitimate IDs, car keys, and money, money, money. Too Cool Moms have also been known to seduce paperboys and prom dates in desperate attempts to alleviate their Ativan-laden depressions.

Aloof Cool

Marked by their absence of language and finesse with weaponry, this is the territory of bounty hunters, rogue cops, and *undercover* undercover agents. Like the Cool Teacher, this cool persona rarely achieves bona fide fame outside of fiction. He's not your mama's John Wayne cowboy—this guy practices "moral flexibility" and if that means fighting dirty then yeah . . . what about it? (A favorite joke demonstrating this principle: "Hey, did you hear that Jack Bauer shot Helen Keller in the kneecaps to make her talk?") Despite his propensity towards graphic sadism, the Aloof Cool only pops kneecaps when absolutely necessary. If this guys ends up shooting your mother in the back, you can be sure she had it coming. This isn't ordinary violence either—this is artful brutality. These guys crack skulls with the finesse of a prima ballerina. And such agility. No matter how tangled up, the dexterous Aloof Cool will find a way to slip out of his ropes, handcuffs, or bear trap. He can load a gun, jimmy a lock, and light a cigarette all at the same time. With the stealth and nine-life endurance of a tomcat, the Aloof Cool can survive roof drops, natural disasters, even the occasional bomb. Like a cartoon feline, he climbs out of the rubble again and again, his charred body shaken yet ready for more.

The Aloof Cool is anti-cerebral. He would no sooner sit down on an analyst's couch to vent about his overbearing mother than he would wax his chest and have a pedicure. Not only is discussing his feelings out of the question, but so is discussing *anything, ever*—to the point where those who encounter him must guess the answers to such unremarkable questions as "Would you like a refill?" or "Do you need an ambulance?" Even when a simple "yes," "no," or "push the red button," could spare him days on end without food, shelter, or appropriate shaving supplies—this diehard still will not utter a single explanatory word.

Outside of Hollywood, the unfamous Aloof Cool is far more fallible and may even miss occasionally when he tosses his trash into the barrel across the room. His self-esteem is so high that those around him wonder if the Aloof Cool has even so much as stubbed a toe. This persona might work well out on the fictional prairies and crime-ridden streets, but it tends to get a little lost in translation when Mr. Aloof shows up at say, a friend's birthday party. He may balk at removing his shoes, be reprimanded for lighting up indoors, and down his Cosmopolitan in a single gulp. Although women are magnetically drawn to him, they sometimes wonder if his lack of engagement might be the result of some speech impediment or limited intelligence. His tricks of agility, like lighting a match with one hand or cracking a bottle open with his teeth, go over like public indigestion. In short, the Aloof Cool is not much of a social animal. His allure is based on the concept of distance—a piercing glance from a subway window. Anonymity is his modus operandi. Sexual encounters are rarely followed up with phone calls, much less second dates. This suits most women just fine, though, because the Aloof Cool cannot be reprogrammed for domestic use.

One distinguishing feature of this cool type is the presence of perpetual five o'clock shadow. This shadow is at times less stubble and more moss, depending on when the aloof one last slipped in a quick shave. This "unbeard" can even resemble an early-stage Chia Pet at times, coining the phenomenon known by some as "Chia face." On screen, the presence of perpetual shadow often defies the laws of time and feasibility. Viewers know, for example, that the aloof one has been on the run for days on end. He has neither eaten nor slept, and is frequently suffering from at least one gunshot wound. Yet the face shadow remains constant from scene to grueling scene, thus implying that the Aloof Cool has managed to land some contraband grooming supplies. There, in his hideaway trashcan or stairwell, we are asked to believe that our vagabond hero has been catching up on his personal

Match the following unbeards to their rightful owners.

1. Jack Bauer (Kiefer Sutherland)   **A.**

2. Jon Locke (Terry O'Quinn)   **B.**

3. Jack Shephard (Matthew Fox)   **C.**

4. Walker, Texas Ranger (Chuck Norris)   **D.**

5. John McClane (Bruce Willis)   **E.**

6. The Man with No Name (Clint Eastwood)   **F.**

7. Sonny Crockett (Don Johnson)   **G.**

8. Mad Max (Mel Gibson)   **H.**

9. Indiana Jones (Harrison Ford)   **I.**

10. Rambo (Sylvester Stallone)   **J.**

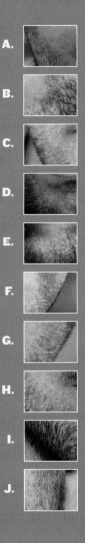

grooming. Even when a legitimate shaving occurs at 9:00 A.M. (as documented on Jack Bauer's *24*-and-counting clock), the shadow is back by the 10:00 A.M. episode. In *Lost*, the castaway he-men manage to pursue child abductors and gigantic warthogs in eternal states of quarter-inch face moss. (Possibly, a grunge salon will soon be discovered on the far side of the island and the secret to the ¼-inch shave will finally be revealed.)

More of the Famous

David Carradine (Kwai Chang Caine) from *Kung Fu*, Harmonica (Charles Bronson) in *Once Upon a Time in the West*, Boba Fett in *The Empire Strikes Back*. See also the *"Match the Unbeard"* section which follows.

Habitat

This is Sergio Leone country, the dugouts and plains of *The Man With No Name*. He can also be found in Mexican whore houses, smoky urban dives, seedy hotel rooms bathed in flashing neon lights, dirty cabs, dark alleys, abandoned warehouses, and loading docks.

Often Mimicked By

Meathead jocks, hostile body builders, and alcoholics who still live home with their domineering mothers. The impersonator's mannerisms may appear stale, over-rehearsed, and straight out of the man-with-no-name play book. Though credit must be given to these ambitious mimics—giving up language is no easy task. Unfortunately, bartenders can only read the body language of authentic Aloof Cools, who are known for their ability to order drinks like JD on the Rocks, with no more than a grunt and telltale nod. When the impersonator tries to telepathically order such drinks the bartender is forced to partake in guessing games of sign language, which makes the impersonator look literally dumb rather than cool.

Hard-Luck Cool

Not just anyone can sing the blues. It's a good thing the Pop Tarts of today don't write their own lyrics because ballads about the rich and rotten might be more than your smoky bar dweller could bear. While hard-luck stories and blues musicians are often synonymous, this cool type embraces anyone—poet, artist, accountant, or scientist—who has overcome hardship and turned that adversity into a life-affirming passion. As the rest of us wax on and on about that impossible kitchen renovation, consider, next time, how your woes might sound set to a standard 12-bar blues form. For example: The Azalea granite counter wasn't buffed (now repeat four times) and the German nickel sink was oversized (repeat four times). If your song sounds stupid, it probably is. Now, think of little Ray Charles. "Even compared to other blacks," Charles recalled, "we were on the bottom of the ladder looking up at everyone else. Nothing below us except the ground." His father had two other families before finally abandoning Ray's mother. When Charles was five, he witnessed his little brother drown to death in a portable laundry tub—this would be one of his last sighted memories as the next year he began to go blind. Completely sightless by seven, Ray wasn't cut any slack at all when it came to his chores. When he tripped over steps with his arms full of firewood or a bucket of well water, his mother insisted, "You may be blind, but you ain't stupid."[9] Hard-Luck Cools, no matter how oppressed, rise up out of the ashes and learn to be resourceful. Writer Donnell Alexander puts it like this:

> "That inclination to make something out of nothing and then to make that something special articulated itself first in the work chants that slaves sang in the field and then in the hymns that rose out of their churches . . . Cool is all about trying to make a dollar out of 15 cents. It's about living on the cusp, on the periphery, diving for scraps."[10]

Most of the founding mothers and fathers of the Blues grew up comparatively poor, often in the segregated South. Biographies abound about mothers who were hookers, paraplegics, or slowly dying of tuberculosis. Fathers, likewise, were either incestuos deadbeats, or deaf, one-armed tobacco pickers. And these were the kids lucky enough *not* to be orphans. Take Louisiana Red, whose mother died of pneumonia when he was seven days old. When Red was five, his father was murdered by the KKK.[11] Talk about earning the right to whine out loud. Less guttural and more academic was the art and poetry of the Harlem Renaissance, which embodied the evolution of black oppression. Langston Hughes was a busboy by day and a poet by night. Abandoned by his father, Langston lived on and off with his struggling mother, but mostly with his self-reliant grandmother—until, of course, she died. While Hughes's childhood was indeed marked by hardship, his poetry embodied the broader struggle of black freedom. It spoke to the dawning black migration— of a people moving beyond the Jim Crow South to urban cultural epicenters like New York and Chicago. The following is an excerpt from his poem "A New Song."

Ray Charles: cut no slack by mama

> Bitter was the day
> When I saw my children unschooled,
> My young men without a voice in the world
> My women taken as the body-toy
> Of a thieving people
> ...*That day is past.*[12]

Woody Guthrie: plagued by fire

Hard-Luck Cools, of course, aren't always black. It isn't easy, but even a white folk musician can qualify. Consider Woody Guthrie, for example, author of the American classic "This Land is Your Land." Already victims of the Dust Bowl droughts, the Guthries lost their house in a tragic fire. Soon after, fire plagued the family again when Woody's little sister set herself aflame (a supposed accident) and burned to death. His mother, meanwhile, was slowly dying from the physically and mentally debilitating Huntington's disease. Woody's father, a known KKK member, had his mother committed to a mental asylum after she supposedly set him—you guessed it—on fire.[13]

No matter how many years these dejected waifs spent scavenging as street urchins or living in footlockers—no matter how epic their struggle, these Hard-Luck Cools became success stories *because* of what they suffered. This is the old "bone heals strongest at the break" principle, or as Nietzsche put it: "What doesn't kill us makes us stronger."[14] Hard-Luck Cools also have that ever-alluring wounded puppy appeal. While in their presence, the average entitled piggy is overwhelmed with compassion. These big-eyed orphans, regardless of their age, gain cool points for merely *surviving* their horrific childhoods, never mind all that uber-high achieving.

The Hard-Luck Cool never whines overtly about his or her compromised beginnings. Sure, there may be a cathartic release that takes place via artistic expression, but never on a therapist's couch. Humility is key to this cool type; blame is for those who wallow in self-pity. The Hard-Luck Cool doesn't want your sympathy. They may, for example, refer to "growing up out of state" and leave it at that. This vagueness is not rooted in shame but a desire to avoid all potential pissing contests over who had the most dysfunctional family. In fact, most Hard-Luck Cools abandon ship as soon as terms like "dysfunctional" and "self-actualization" enter into the conversation.

More of the Famous

Actual: Abraham Lincoln, Muddy Waters, Memphis Minnie, Robert Johnson, Son House, Countee Cullen, Judy Garland, James Brown, Devin Hester, Lawrence Krisna Parker, Loretta Lynn, Frank McCourt. *Fictitious*: Chris Gardner (Will Smith) in *The Pursuit of Happyness* (based on a true story).

Habitat

One-room shacks, whorehouses, tenement apartments, overcrowded orphanages, vaudeville greenrooms, roadhouses.

Often Mimicked By

Well-to-do narcissists who have *never* really endured hardship or those who actually *have* endured hardship and never shut-up about it. Unfortunately, many who suffer early in life grow up to be unkind humans or even twisted sadists. Others, like Vanilla Ice, invent hard luck stories, to manufacture an otherwise non-existent street cred. Similarly, a slew of fabricated memoirs have been the cause of recent controversies in the publishing industry. Certainly, the secondhand nature of literature makes it vulnerable to the practice of ego stroking. James Frey, author of *A Million Little Pieces* details his battle against "the fury" of drug and alcohol addiction. The book documents a whirlwind account of mowing down cops, masochistic dentistry, and turbo-charged crack abuse. For better or for worse, Frey made a lot of it up.[15] Another faker extraordinaire is Bruno Grosjean whose memoir chronicled a horrendous concentration camp childhood; it turned out that Grosjean wasn't even Jewish much less a Holocaust survivor.[16] Or Margaret Seltzer whose LA "gang" memoir was recently outed as a total fiction. Not only has Margaret never been a foster child or run drugs for the "bloods," but she's a well-to-do graduate of a private Episcopal day school.[17] It's difficult to know exactly what psychological deficit motivates authors to reinvent themselves as less privileged others. Many of us, no doubt, would enjoy sympathy from strangers, for crowds of people to punch the air as we strolled by their bus stops or lunch tables, though it takes above-average arrogance to lie with such resolve.

Queen of Cool

These boys are over the top and damn proud of it. Maybe as youngsters they were scorned for dressing up in gold lamé, but as adults, their flamboyant wardrobes only add to their inexorable appeal. Overt camp says, "I am fearless" like little else. A man in sequins and fishnets is a raspberry in the face of every fag-mashing bully. It takes guts to act out those repressed dress-up fantasies—and this is why the Queens of Cool are never guilty of Trying Too Hard (though *trying an awful lot* is a given when it comes to drag). To see a man, any man, so happy in size-12 platform boots is a testament to the human spirit. Why? Because we know that most gay men have suffered the stigma of the ridiculed outsider. The degree of suffering usually depends on what decade and what geographic area the Queen of Cool grew up in. This history of marginalization earns the brave queen a certain badge of honor.

While most Queens of Cool are gay men, some choose to remain "undeclared." A few are even seemingly straight. There is, most certainly, an alluring mystique surrounding the sexually ambiguous male. That "does he or doesn't he" aura can keep the masses guessing. And what female, after all, can resist the anomaly of a fashionable man who sleeps with women *and* listens to all their secrets? But what, precisely, makes the Queen of Cool, cool? Is it his capacity to summon desire in even the most macho of straight men? His uncanny ability to look better in women's clothes than most women? His unabashed exhibitionism? Yes, yes, and yes, but the quality that yields more cool than any other is the queen's unwavering confidence. For here is a man so deeply immersed in his true sexual essence that being anything other than the rare bird he is would be a crime against nature.

Though gay acceptance has no doubt made huge strides in recent decades, the swishy queen will continue to rile feathers in many social strata. Even today with the likes of Carson from *Queer Eye*—seeing a gay man strut his stuff in public still echoes of insubordination. Witnessing such a brazen act of social defiance can be unexpectedly inspiring. This may be why those in the presence of performing Queens of Cool often jump from their chairs with outbursts such as "Lordy mama "or "Amen sister!" And even if a rampant homophobe does manage to slip into the audience, he or she will likely be singled out by the queen's phobe-detector and summarily *made an example of.*

Homage must be paid here to the 70s glam rockers who paved the way for future Queens of Cool. In the days of ubiquitous queer-whacking, rockers like Marc Bolan, David Bowie, and Freddie Mercury dared to go where few omnisexuals had ever gone before. While the folkies made due with rugged jeans, dirty T-shirts and that single, all-purpose bandanna, these glamour boys were getting Merle Norman makeovers and stocking up on lingerie. And who could resist Marc Bolan with his feather boas and glittered cheekbones? Or Freddie Mercury, father of the unitard—to imagine rock history *without* the unitard is nothing short of blasphemy. Sporting a unitard, of course, requires a unique brand of courage. These rockers, after all, were not known for their buff physiques—most looked less like Popeye and more like Olive Oyl. Ziggy Stardust's legs were about the same circumference as his biceps, which were about the same circumference as his microphone. Glam rats like Bowie weren't trying to be sexy so much as innovative. How else to describe that flaming orange mullet with complementary arm warmers?

Of course, not all Queens of Cool are fantastically famous. While the desire for fame is implicit in this cool type, most stadium/encore fantasies go unrealized. More likely, the burgeoning Queen of Cool spends night after adolescent night pantomiming Tim Curry in front of the full-length mirror on his locked bedroom door. At dinner, when mother inquires about her missing pair of fishnets, the queen-in-training may stare down at his mashed potatoes and blush. So what *does* become of all those

Match the Camp Accessory

1. Elton John

2. Liberace

3. Little Richard

4. Mick Jagger

5. Jake Shears

6. Michael Jackson

7. Boy George

8. Adam Ant

9. Tim Curry

A. pomade pompadour

B. stripey-tard

C. uniglove

D. banana hammock

E. war paint

F. top hat

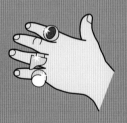

G. bling rings

H. rhinestone platforms

I. leather corset

Answers: 1=H, 2=G, 3=A, 4=B, 5=D, 6=C, 7=F, 8=E, 9=I

glamour boys who never show up on the cover of the *Rolling Stone*? You can find them out there on dance floors across the nation, voguing their hearts out. These are the guys you can't look away from—the ones who take Christmas parties by storm, give karaoke a good name, and make community theater a worthwhile public service.

Habitat
Tour buses, dressing rooms, arena catwalks, locked bedrooms, karaoke bars, dance floors, parade floats, community theater.

Often Mimicked By
Macho-glams, headbangers, and the vampire obsessed. So is every man with the guts to wear a unitard a Queen of Cool? Absolutely not, particularly those who look too good in them. The Lycra inclination must be rooted in audacity rather than vanity. The Queen wears the unitard not to be sexy, but because it's better to dance in and the closest thing to being naked. For example, metal rockers who sport the elastic crotch as a means of accentuating their suspiciously huge packages of manhood—these are not Queens of Cool. This macho school of glam may be likened to the "maybian" phenomenon among woman. Maybians are straight woman who pose as lesbians to shock and awe (e.g., the Britney/Madonna kiss). Likewise, macho-glams like Paul Stanley and Gene Simmons (of KISS fame) display overtly homosexual

Freddie Mercury: father of the unitard

gestures as a means of riling up controversy. Ironically, heavy metal does not have a gay friendly reputation. Perhaps the worst example of this was when Sebastian Bach (of Skid Row) appeared on MTV wearing a T-shirt that read "AIDS Kills Fags Dead."[18] Though Mötley Crüe drummer Tommy Lee did confess, in an interview with *Blender* magazine, that a man had groped him while they were high on ecstasy. "Maybe," Tommy admitted, "if he was *really* good looking I may have *slightly* considered it."[19] The groper, unfortunately, was not his type.

Wild-Woman Cool

These are the girls who put princesses to shame. Like Queens of Cool, this personality type is all about breaking the gender mold. No bimbos, gold diggers, or raunch mongers here. No virginal girls-next-door either. While many may refer to them as "bad girls," "radical" better describes their credo. These women aren't waiting around to be saved by any dim-witted prince—in fact, men are often of limited use to them. You won't catch them in do-me pumps either, droning on and on about the scarcity of straight marriageable men. If they *are* single, no one told them it was a social condition on par with leprosy. While marriage and children may be part of their plan, so is tipping over the patriarchy and shaking down the Christian Right.

Sometimes, these rad-girls are accused of being angry lesbians—even when they're straight. The "angry lesbian" charge is levied whenever a Wild Woman does something "unbecoming." For example, when the bald Sinead O'Connor ripped a picture of the pope in half on live TV, she was called not only an angry lesbian but a pariah and a witch. Rather than ask Ms. O'Connor why she did what she did, angry Americans booed her off stages and smashed her tapes under steamrollers. Turns out, Sinead was protesting the church hierarchy and its complicity/tolerance of pedophile priests in 1992.[20] In light of the recent U.S. church sex scandals, this Wild Woman looks less like a witch and more like a fortune-teller.

Bad-girl publicity stunts are never part of this cool type's agenda. Not that Wild Women don't drum up publicity; they often do. But media attention is the by-product of their actions, not the intention. The Guerrilla Girls, for instance, are artful activists who dress up in gorilla masks to expose wrongful practices, according to their website:

> "We're feminist masked avengers in the tradition of anonymous do-gooders like Robin Hood, Wonder Woman and Batman. How do we expose sexism, racism and corruption in politics, art, film, and pop culture? With facts, humor, and outrageous visuals. We reveal the understory, the subtext, the overlooked, and the downright unfair."[21]

In 2002 they put up a highly visible billboard in Hollywood that read "The Anatomically Correct Oscar" A white, rather than gold version of the Oscar statue was pictured with more text below: "He's white and male, just like the guys who win." Also cited was the fact that no woman has *ever* won for Best Director and that merely three percent of Oscars are awarded to people of color. The stunt received big publicity, articles in *The Los Angeles Times, The Sunday Herald, London, BBC Online, Salon* and others. The Guerilla Girls were featured (in their Gorilla masks) on *Access*

Hollywood, NBC-TV, and CBS-TV. This was rebellion with a cause, an action to make a statement, not simply a publicity stunt to grab tabloid headlines. That year, the first African-American, Halle Berry, won the Oscar for Best Actress.

Wild-Woman divas blaze their own trails. Often by default, these trails become the gateways to transformative trends. Grace Jones brought androgyny to new heights back in the 80s. Her outrageous power suits and flattop Afro inspired an entire decade of unisex power dressing. This woman has done everything from pissing off Disney (she's banned from Walt's properties worldwide) to singing duets with Pavarotti to benefit Angolan refugees.[22] Or indy-pioneer Ani DiFranco, who decided, at eighteen, that she didn't want her career under any record company's thumb so she started her own, "Righteous Babe Records." Vintage fashion queen, Cyndi Lauper had a day job at Screaming Mimi's New York Thrift Shop. When she made it big, this diva took her one-of-a-kind wardrobe with her, and by 1985 every teenage girl in America had at least three retro getups in her closet, rhinestones included.

Not every Wild Woman gets to cast her mother in her smash hit music video like Cyndi Lauper did. A lot of Wild Women have no interest in stardom whatsoever because stardom is a pain in the ass, and Wild Women are not known for their capacity to put up with the trite and superficial. These anonymous renegades are often drawn to man-centric careers where they eventually earn the respect and admiration of their male coworkers. They may also be biker chicks, but not of the hog-back-bitch variety. No, Wild-Woman Cools drive their own bikes, their own cars, their own careers, and their own investment portfolios.

More of the Famous

Actual: Mae West, Eartha Kitt, Margaret Cho, Roseanne Barr, Lea Delaria. *Fictitious*: Thelma (Geena Davis) and Louise (Susan Sarandon) in *Thelma and Louise*.

Habitat

The open road, indy recording studios, court, thrift shops, picket lines.

Often Mimicked By

Spring Break tarts and manufactured celebrities. The diva, of late, has been increasingly associated with the "girls gone wild" phenomenon. This brand of diva follows the very predictable "rocky road" to stardom: dysfunctional family estrangement, leaked sex tape, DWIs, "tasteful" centerfold, ill-fated stints in rehab, etc. This attention-getting behavior should never be confused with genuine Wild-Woman Cool. To differentiate, here are a few things a Wild-Woman Cool would never do: reality TV, shop drunk, marry after the fourth drink.

Politi-Cool

These are the intellectual cools that can rattle statistics off the tops of their heads as if reading from a teleprompter—even when they're not. These are the *West Wing* quippers who tell ironic jokes about Yeats, Kafka, and lame-duck sessions. In meetings they may apologize for "taking this call," then suddenly break into fluent Russian, Chinese, or Farsi. Don't try to debate these brainiacs; they are masters of spin and the subtleties of language. Besides, they drop counterpoints like bombs, blowing all your sensible arguments to smithereens. But make no mistake; these Politi-Cools are not the same stiff-collared elitists whose portraits dominate the hallways of golf clubs and statehouses. No cigar chewing Good Ol' Boys here. If these quippers did come out of the Ivy League, most likely, they landed there on scholarships. Social service is the Politi-Cool's aspiration and public policy is the means to that end. These cool types resist politics-as-usual back-scratching, yet their skills in "creative" negotiation are widely admired. They are in it for the humanitarian buzz, the posterity, and maybe even a page or two in the history books of the future. (Also, a statue might be nice, something along the lines of the Lincoln Memorial?)

The Politi-Cool's talents extend beyond the marble halls of government cathedrals. These rascals have been known to belt out hair-raising jazz riffs on the woodwinds or electric guitars. In fact, if Tony Blair had been slightly more talented, he might have just made it as front man for his band "The Ugly Rumours." Back in the day, Tony's gig-wear consisted of Cuban heels and a flesh-revealing trumpet-sleeve shirt.[23] His style, apparently, was dance-spastic, very Mick Jagger. While Tony's fearless body language may have contributed to the band's demise, it no doubt added to his mystique as Britain's prime minister. Bill Clinton, of course, was dubbed "America's first black president" after his sax solo brought down the house on *The Arsenio Hall Show*. And of course, there is Barack Obama, current grand poobah of all Politi-Cools. Here's a guy that graced the cover of *Vibe Magazine's* "Juice" issue. Another hipster publication, *Paper*, recently devoted an entire fashion editorial to "Obamawear." The feature was called "Mr. President" and it featured tall, thin black men in slightly too-large suits. Kim Hastreiter, the magazine's co-founder and editor explained the Obama cool-quotient like this:

> *"Many men (especially not politicians!) don't have the ease and personal style and confidence that I see in a man like Barack Obama. Casual yet board-room ready without being too formal or intimidating. He just seems to look comfy in his own skin."*[24]

Bill Clinton, bringing down the house

Mike Huckabee: Politi-Cool or Gomer Pyle gone wild?

Like so many rockers, the Politi-Cool is too often weak, legless even, when it comes to groupie chicks. Often, this vulnerability is the Achilles' heel of his political career. Here the question must be asked: might a career in Metal Rock have better served the Politi-Cool's sexual appetite? Possibly, yet this is the one arena where the righteous public servant gets to be a little bad—a trade-off for the rock star he never became.

This category, like most affairs of state, tends to be male-dominated. Yet occasionally, female politicians do enter the echelons of cool. Vanguard feminists like the charismatic Bella Abzug paved the way with her big, groovy hats and outspoken opinions. The late, brave Benazir Bhutto, like Martin Luther King, fought for her people, despite repeated assassination attempts. Recently, a new wave of leftie hotties has stolen the spotlight. French Socialist Ségolène Royal, for example, or Cristina Fernandez de Kirchner, the new Evita of Argentina. This particular wave of estrogen began at the southern tip of South America when Chile elected Michelle Bachelet. Often these women tend to be conservative in personal style like Hillary Clinton or Nancy Pelosi, even when their politics are liberal. These power dames, unlike their male counterparts, cannot dabble in sexual misadventures lest they be deemed bad girls or menopausal psychopaths. Even though they might not be seducing their interns or laying down drum solos in dark sunglasses, these women maintain their cool where Politi-Cool matters most: the debate podium—because nothing makes a female candidate cooler than the ability to talk a perspiring male opponent into a state of visible panic.

There are two ways, of course, to infiltrate the system: from *inside out* and *outside in*. Conservative media pundits like Bill O'Reilly and Rush Limbaugh can even get militant lefties second-guessing positions such as war, abortion, or global warming. Liberals who dare to enter this perilous domain must prepare to be publicly disemboweled. In a matter of seconds these persuasive bullies can reduce the meek and starving idealist into a sniveling ball of tears. The poor, fragmented, and disorganized Left has failed to match these pundits head to head with its own versions of similarly-styled TV and radio programs. At least the liberals have been able to laugh, which ironically, has evolved into its own political strategy. Political comedies like Jon Stewart's *The Daily Show* and Stephen Colbert's *The Colbert Report* have turned right-wing politics on its head. Stewart and Colbert are cocky, irreverent, and seemingly untouchable, and what could be cooler than that? It's hard to say who was braver, the White House for inviting Stephen Colbert to speak at the 2006 Correspondence Dinner, or Colbert for accepting. The fake right-wing pundit delivered a roast so scathing that George and Laura nearly slithered under their tablecloth. This was Colbert's concept of "truthiness" in full frontal assault and, *man*, was it ugly. Colbert remained cool throughout, delivering one barbed zinger after another while the dumbstruck audience sat silent, not sure whether to laugh, cry, or crawl under the tables themselves. Before that dinner, few aside from Hugo Chavez had so courageously stuck it straight to the Dubbya.

More of the Famous

On the Left: Al Franken, Janeane Garofalo, Rachel Maddow, Keith Olbermann. *On the Right:* Arnold "The Governator" Schwarzenegger, Ann Coulter, Michelle Malkin.

Habitat

Union rallies, New Hampshire diners, the set of *West Wing*, power-lunching at Duke Zeibert's, YouTube, *David Letterman/Jay Leno/Conan O'Brien Shows.*

Often Mimicked By

Ex-wrestlers and retired Navy SEALS. While the decorum of characters like Lincoln is no longer essential for a politician to hold office, some have taken this leeway to outrageous extremes. When former pro-wrestler Jesse Ventura was elected governor of Minnesota, he ended his inaugural address with the much criticized Navy SEAL war cry "*Hoo*Yah!" Similarly, when Howard Dean let out his famous scream, he found out the hard way that "over the top" and charismatic are not one and the same. In fact, this kick-ass school of politics reeks of Trying Too Hard, often compensating for substance with contrived outrageousness. *The Jerry Springer Show* or the WWF circuit is fine for those desperately seeking attention, but the political arena is the last place to work out those fear-of-abandonment issues. With big money the most crucial asset in running for positions of leadership, egocentric personalities have flocked to public office like never before. Yet when Baptist minister Mike Huckabee whips out his electric guitar, the effect is more *Gomer Pyle Gone Wild* than hip politician. Power, like cool, is tainted by every dollar spent in its pursuit. Red flags may include: Choosing *Whole Lotta Love* as campaign song, debating in Bono glasses, and addressing the press as "dudes."

Underdog Cool

Even Hollywood is on to this phenomenon with its recent splurge of films and shows about nerdy outsiders like *Napoleon Dynamite, Ugly Betty,* and *Chuck.* Cool happened to the nerdy Hush Puppy too, a well-known fashion *don't* which suddenly, in the mid-Nineties, (with no help from advertisers), began to skyrocket in popularity. The same thing happened to horn-rimmed glasses and granny sweaters in the late eighties. There is something almost religious in the transformation of the hopelessly uncool. Our sympathies lie with the underdog, for who better deserves a moment in the sun?

At least part of the reason that underdogs have come into fashion has to do with the rise, of reality TV. The premise and draw for many of these shows is laughing *at,* rather than *with,* the would-be entertainer. *The Gong Show* of the 70's was one of the first to put the spotlight on the all-American, beggin'-for-attention whack job. At the time, the show was widely criticized. The Roman Catholic Archdiocese of New York put it on its list of worst programs for children, claiming, "The entire thrust is to demean and ridicule its guests while furnishing a platform for the crude and vulgar comments of host, Chuck Barris."[25] The movie based on Barris's life *Confessions of a Dangerous*

Mind features a Playboy Mansion party scene where Barris, strolling by the pool, is recognized by a beautiful naked swimmer. She approached him, not to seduce him but to heap scorn on him:

> "I think you're the most insidious, despicable force in entertainment today. How dare you subject the rest of the world to your loathsome views of humanity, to mock some poor lonely people who are just craving a little attention in their lives?"[26]

The Gong Show: *deemed crude and vulgar by Catholic Archdiocese.*

Little did anyone back in the 70's know just how low the bar for reality TV could and would go. With an endless supply of people willing to humiliate themselves, and no shortage of producers dreaming up new opportunities to do so, reality TV has become the dirty underwear of our culture.

They line up with their hula-hoops and crackwhore mothers, their horrible voices and their cottage-cheese thighs—"Judge us," they beg. Yet our hearts break as we watch that callous verdict come down—those delusions of grandeur blown to kingdom come. But what, pray tell, can possibly save them? Enter *The Cult Following!* When William Hung belted out his off-key rendition of "She Bangs," *American Idol* judge Simon Cowell lambasted his audition performance: "You can't sing, you can't dance, so what do you want me to say?" To which Hung graciously responded, "Um...I already

William Hung: has no regrets

gave my best, and I have no regrets at all."[27] While Hung never made it to further *Idol* rounds, he did land appearances on *Letterman, Ellen DeGeneres, Dateline, The Early Show* and others. He was also offered a $25,000 record deal, despite rumors (a la Beatles) that the star is dead.

Hung, an engineering student at UC Berkley, is not dead, however. He is one of many geekish curiosities who has risen to the status of cultural demigod. He represents all the *American Idol* throwaways—every guy who's been laughed in the face for asking a beautiful woman to dance. The public loves him for his drastic uncoolness, because it never occurred to this lovable loser that he wasn't talented or beautiful enough to play with his genetic superiors. And this innocent contradiction actually makes the uncool curiously cool. Geeks get even cooler, and fast, when a technical crisis comes along. The ability to reboot that 8-port router is every bit as seductive as any second-hand version of "Hot Blooded." Desperate women have been known to greet Geek Squad cowboys in heels and satin teddies—the same women who laughed 10 years ago when that geek had asked them to dance.

More of the Famous
Actual: Andy Kaufman, Michael Essany. *Fictitious:* Rudolph the Red-Nosed Reindeer, Peter Parker (Tobey Maguire) in *Spiderman*, Gomer Pyle (Jim Nabors) from *The Andy Griffith Show*, Forrest Gump (Tom Hanks), Bill Haverchuck (Martin Starr) from *Freaks and Geeks*, Radar O'Riley (Gary Burghoff) from *M*A*S*H*.

Habitat
Public high schools, reality TV, science fairs, Geek Squad Volkswagens.

Often Mimicked By
"Ugly ducklings" and 98-pound weaklings. Hollywood loves an ugly-duckling story. Problem is, putting a pair of glasses on a beautiful girl does not make her an ugly duckling. These films inevitably stumble through scene after scene of the ugly

duckling in unfashionable potato-sack clothes being shunned by her heartless peers. After endless humiliations (which usually include wiping out in the school cafeteria), the "homely" slob is finally discovered and transformed via the wonders of makeover technology into a swan. Real underdogs *do* get tortured, yet no amount of lip liner is going to reverse their fortunes. Enduring social ridicule is often what earns the underdog his or her badge of honor. It takes more than a mere physical transformation, even through diet and plastic surgery, to render the underdog cool. The boy version, of course, is the 98-pound-weakling story. This premise is at least more authentic to the laws of cool because the weak one often takes up esteem-building pursuits such as karate, step dancing, or saving the planet. In the end, he has something more than a makeover to show for himself.

Too-Sexy Cool

These lyrics to Right Said Fred's one-hit-wonder say it all:

I'm too sexy for my car too sexy for my car
Too sexy by far
And I'm too sexy for my hat
Too sexy for my hat what do you think about that

Why "Too Sexy" and not just sexy enough? Because such a condition actually exists. These hot ones exude sexuality like water from a fire hose—and they don't need to pole-dance in lingerie to do it. The Too-Sexy object has been known to cause car accidents and heart palpitations. This cool type is not synonymous with traditional beauty, which comes with every advantage. Sexy transcends beauty—sexy is about essence.

Match the Sexy Attribute

1. Elvis Presley

2. Joan Jett

3. Marlon Brando

4. Michael Hutchence

5. Chrissy Hynde

6. Bruce Springsteen

7. Betty Grable

8. Meryl Streep

9. Lou Reed

10. Kurt Cobain

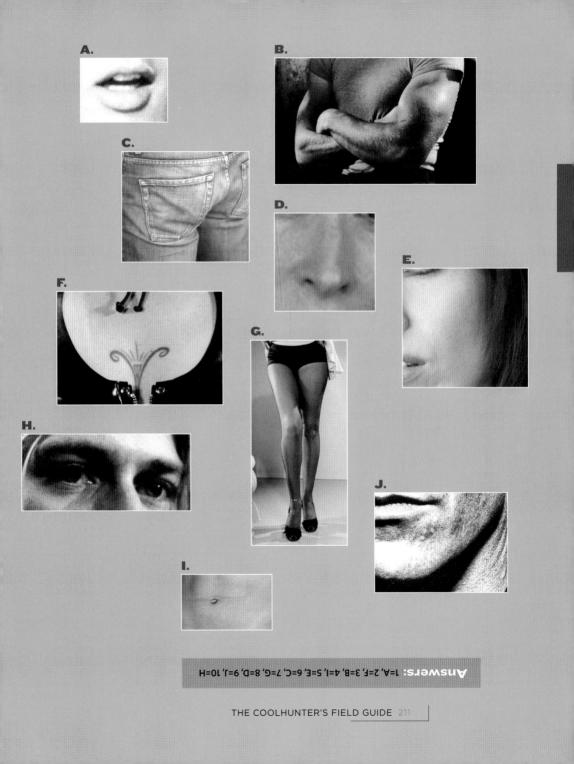

A.

B.

C.

D.

E.

F.

G.

H.

J.

I.

Male Too-Sexy's are famous for their shriek-provoking abilities. In the concert hall, the collective sound made by hysterical teenage girls has been compared to a Harrier Jet taking off. A particular performance, in fact, can be gauged for sex appeal based on shriek volume alone. A gesture as subtle as tucking a hair-chunk behind an ear can instantly triple the decibels. Too-Sexy Cools have been known to hypnotize entire arenas into semiconscious state of emotional rapture. Swooning, as opposed to shrieking, involves weeping, air-hugging, and incessant reaching—such power, all induced by the animal magnetism of a single man or woman. If harnessed, this energy could power up rocket boosters.

Too-Sexy performers frequently possess a single irresistible mannerism or physical attribute which works in concert with other cool qualities such as inordinate talent, understated confidence, and uncanny coordination. Below is a list of signature physical attributes along with a list of the famous that exhibit them.

Habitat
Armored limos, rear exits, remote getaways, inside security barricades.

Often Mimicked By
Self-proclaimed sex god/goddesses. Madonna's *Sex* book did not make her any sexier and many considered it her greatest career embarrassment. When Rod Stewart sang "Do Ya Think I'm Sexy?" more than a few replied emphatically, "Not anymore!" Sexy, in order to be cool, must appear effortless, accidental even—as if the "cursed" would be less sexy—if only they could help it. Overtly sexual fashions are fine for turning tricks, but beyond this, they tend to imply a certain desperation. And porn is just porn—anyone can rip off their clothes for a camera. With sex in all its permutations being used to sell us everything from air fresheners to car tires, the viewing public is suffering from T&A fatigue. Too-Sexy Cool is never *in yer face*; like great wine, this brand of cool needs time to settle onto the palate.

The Coolhunter's Field Guide: Conclusion

Rarely does a cool one fit seamlessly into any single category. Elvis, for example, had that lip thing as well as coming from nothing, and, yes, he did love that rhinestone bodysuit, which, theoretically *could* be deemed a unitard. He's got hard luck roots with a dash of queen, and a whole lot of sexy. Again, these distinctions by type are simply guidelines for differentiating the cool we already know. Most of the cool categories mentioned above share a certain confidence—that alluring self-awareness so easily associated with cool. "Naming that cool" helps us understand its evolutionary quirks in relation to ever-changing cultural environments. How, for example, did the Harlem Renaissance define the cool of its day? Did the harsh climate of today's reality TV prepare the way for the recent wave of Underdog Cools? Classifying cool also points out those pockets of the human psyche where cool tends to collect: the exhibitionist, the leader, the artist, the survivor, etc. These are the breeding grounds of cool; investigating their origins may not be up there with cracking the genome, but it succeeds in removing *at least a few* layers of its mystery.

Cool

CONCLUSION

Cool is an all-encompassing phenomenon. It's everywhere we go—the crux of nearly every advertisement we see. Few undertakings consume our modern lives more than the incessant pursuit of cool. It's is the ephemeral gold standard; without such distinctions, the culturally ambitious would be without benchmarks, floundering in a sea of aesthetic ambiguity. Maybe, you may reasonably conclude, we have too much time on our hands. But cool has been around before the mass marketing of material goods. It was there in the way that particular caveman slung his bear-hide sack over his shoulder. That Aztec mom had it—the one that all the other Aztec moms wanted to hang with. There were, no doubt, Politi-cools in Roman times, and Queens of Cool in ancient Egypt. For all we know, the Aloof Cool persona might trace back to an ancient Nordic tribe with limited language skills yet remarkable finesse with the ironhead spear. And they, too, might have had an affinity for the quarter-inch beard, grooming their man moss with razor-sharp stones. The legendary Amazon she-warriors not only inspired Greek mythology, but Joan of Arc and generations of Wild Women to come. Even the great philosophers debated the dilemmas of cool. Antisthenes, a live-simple hippie type, was famous for "faking poverty" by dressing below his means—a habit that Socrates saw through in more ways than one. "I can see your vanity, Antisthenes, through the holes in your cloak."[1] Socrates' wisdom, of course, applies to modern day wangsters and bohemian wannabes as well.

Cool is undoubtedly a criterion for mate selection. When the dance floor clears and that one guy is left to robot his heart out, he's there for one of two reasons: because he's that good, or because he's that bad. The good robot, no doubt, is the envy of all and will have his choice of dance/sex partners later on. But what about that other guy, the bad robot? Here is where cool gets a little tricky. Remember, the crowd is mesmerized—watching a bad dancer is every bit as entertaining as watching a good one. Why? Because he's brave. Because he couldn't care less if he's cool or not—and this in itself is admirably cool. By this principle, many geeks, nerds or other stereotypes that previously embodied the uncool archetype, have now risen to the status of cool. This geek/underdog cool is obviously very different from the classic "Fonzie" cool. While sex partners may still be harder to come by, the underdog can at least bask in this new revision of the status quo: it's cool to be uncool.

Of course, no one wants to be caught scraping the "new" out of their $500 dollar leather jacket, or standing on line at the pharmacy with a tube of Rogaine in one hand and a nose hair trimmer in the other—who wants to be caught with their cool pants literally down around their ankles? Yet, despite the obvious hazards, the quest for cool is immune to rational thought. No other human attribute is more alluring, not even beauty. Cool, hands down, trumps beauty because even an old toad can be cool—because cool does not discriminate against age, sex, race, or persuasion. What other advertising ploy can be used to sell products to preadolescents and geriatrics alike? Yet, according to youth-centric marketing firms like Look Look, only two to three percent of the entire population is categorized as innately possessing cool. These few "innovators"—as the industry often terms them—have no inclination to seek out cool in the form of material goods, leaving behind, of course, the other ninety-seven-and-a-half percent that are. And are they ever. With so many hucksters so aggressively pressuring the public to buy into *their* version of cool, the modern consumer may feel our cultural aesthetic reduced to the level of a junior-high bathroom fight. Since when did large corporations earn the right to lecture anyone on the principles of cool? The Man, it turns out, is still The Man, despite his hipster makeover. What he sells is the promise of cool, a promise with all the guaranteed satisfaction of the Amazing All-American Sea Monkey. So the next time that bullhorn is inches from your ear, blaring out the latest commandments of cool—pause for a minute and think: just who, really, is more likely to come out on top? When the music stops, who's left holding that pair of leather pants?

Geek, dweeb, emo, or sensitive artist—despite your stereotype or recent brain scan, you're most likely a lot cooler than you think. You may miss every time you try to throw that crushed beer can into the trash barrel. Maybe you can't even crush the damn can. But the trick is to embrace your uncool self. Many a life-affirming moment has been sacrificed for fear of being uncool. For example, in the frozen food aisle, you may be tempted to bust into your best robot (albeit rusty) because that piped-in Motown went down deep. And why shouldn't you let your freak flag fly? The fear of looking stupid never held back the likes of Jim Carrey or Robin Williams. As this book states over and over, nothing taints cool more than its obsessive pursuit. Be forewarned: relentless cool-checking may generate states of neurotic self-consciousness, as if reality TV judges are ruthlessly critiquing your every move. Find the integrity to shut those voices out. Real cool is what happens when you're caught in the act of being yourself—in the hum that occasionally exists between you and the big weird world around you. It may not happen every day, or even every month, but every now and then that beer can *will* land in the barrel, crushed or not. Or, you *will* robot, right there in frozen foods, and, for at least three seconds, you—with your cool face on— will be the definitive sharp note in the universal opus.

And what more, really, could any poor slob hope for?

Endnotes

Introduction

[1] Pauline Weston Thomas, Fashion-era.com "Beauty is Shape" http://www.fashion-era.com/beauty_is_shape.htm (Accessed December 29, 2007)

[2] Pauline Weston Thomas, Fashion-era.com "The Aesthetic Dress Movement: Fashion History of Aesthetics" http://www.fashion-era.com/aesthetics.htm (Accessed December 28, 2007)

Part I: The History of Cool

[1] Pauline Weston Thomas, Fashion-era.com "Beauty is Shape" http://www.fashion-era.com/beauty_is_shape.htm (Accessed December 29, 2007)

[2] "The History of the Barbarians: Vikings" http://www.wizardrealm.com/barbarians/vikings.html (Accessed December 28, 2007)

[3] Margaret Moser, *Movie Stars Do the Dumbest Things,* Renaissance Books, Milwaukee, WI, 1st edition, 1999.

[4] Lawrence Rosenwald. "The Theory, Practice & Influence of Thoreau's Civil Disobedience" William Cain, ed. *A Historical Guide to Henry David Thoreau.* Cambridge: Oxford University Press, 2006.

[5] Ralph Waldo Emerson, "The American Scholar" delivered in Cambridge, August 1837, published by The Laurentian Press, New York 1901

[6] Susan Cheevers (2006). *American Bloomsbury: Louisa May Alcott, Ralph Waldo Emerson, Margaret Fuller, Nathaniel Hawthorne, and Henry David Thoreau; Their Lives, Their Loves, Their Work.* Detroit: Thorndike Press. Large print edition. p. 104. ISBN 078629521X.

[7] Nathaniel Hawthorne, *The Blithdale Romance,* Caxton Society, 1852, page 79

[8] Normandy & Sussex, "Charleston" http://www.gardensnormandysussex.com/uk/garden_detail.aspx?Venue=4 (Accessed December 29, 2007)

[9] Mike Zerwin, "The Prince of Silence" *Sons of Miles Series,* Culture Kiosque, JAZZNET http://www.culturekiosque.com/jazz/miles/rhemiles2.htm (Accessed December 30, 2007)

[10] Tina Gianoulis, "Charlie Parker" *St. James Encyclopedia of Pop Culture,* Gale Group, 2002 http://findarticles.com/p/articles/mi_g1epc/is_bio/ai_2419200930 (Accessed January 2, 2008)

11 PBS American Masters website http://www.pbs.org/wnet/americanmasters/database/parker_c.html (Accessed January 3, 2008)

12 Jazz Extra, "Lester Young Biography" http://www.jazzextra.com/biographies/lester-young.php (Accessed January 3, 2008)

13 "Ella Fitzgerald Biography" Just the Swing, History of Swing http://www.just-the-swing.com/bio/ella-fitzgerald (Accessed January 3, 2008)

14 James Auburn, "Billie Holiday: The Lady Who Sang and Lived the Blues" http://www.musicbizadvice.com/billie_holiday_rediscovered_talent.htm (Accessed January 5, 2008)

15 Jack Kerouac, *On the Road*, 1957, Penguin Classics, 1991, Penguin Group USA

16 Ibid.

17 Ewin Ritchie Elmont, "What Capote Said About Kerouac" *The New York Times*, Oct 25, 1992 http://query.nytimes.com/gst/fullpage.html?res=9E0CEFDF113FF936A15753C1A964958260 (Accessed January 10, 2008)

18 Don Ackers, "On the Road, Criticism" Answers.com http://www.answers.com/topic/on-the-road-novel-7 (Accessed, January 12, 2008)

19 Ibid.

20 "The John Lennon I Knew" from the *Telegraph*.co.uk, October 5, 2005 http://www.telegraph.co.uk/arts/main.jhtml?xml=/arts/2005/10/05/bmlennon05.xml (Accessed January 15, 2008)

21 Timothy Leary, *Chaos and Cyberculture* "Hippies From A to Z" http://www.hipplanet.com/books/atoz/activism.htm (Accessed January 16, 2008)

22 "Kanye West: White People Should Like White Music," contactmusic.com http://www.contactmusic.com/new/xmlfeed.nsf/mndwebpages/kanye%20west%20white%20people%20should%20make%20white%20music (Accessed January 18, 2008)

23 Kitwana, Bakari. *The Hip Hop Generation: Young Blacks and the Crisis in African American Culture,* Basic Civitas Books, page 282.

24 Graham Keeley, "Gay Victims of Franco Era to Win Compensation" *The Independent*, Dec 28, 2006 http://news.independent.co.uk/europe/article2108206.ece (Accessed January 12, 2008)

25 Locksley Hall, "Vaguely Gay, From David Bowie to Jared Leto" AfterElton.com http://www.afterelton.com/music/2006/6/vaguelygay.html (Accessed January 16, 2008)

26 "On MSNBC, Coulter Called Gore a 'Total Fag' While Chris Matthews Said 'We'd Love to Have Her Back.'" MediaMatters for America, July 27, 2006 http://mediamatters.org/items/200607280001 (Accessed January 16, 2008)

27 Sarah Hall, "Isaiah Enters Treatment", "E!" news online, Wed, 24 Jan 2007 http://www.eonline.com/news/article/index.jsp?uuid=4ee83ebf-86dd-494c-a015-fd9bdf5f78e2 (Accessed Jan 19, 2008)

28 Memorable quotes for *Thank You for Smoking* (2005)

http://www.imdb.com/title/tt0427944/ (Accessed January 11, 2008)

29 "Lung Cancer and Smoking Statistics" Cancer Research UK
http://info.cancerresearchuk.org/cancerstats/types/lung/smoking/ (Accessed January 15, 2008)

30 James Neill, "Otzi, the 5,300 Year Old Iceman from the Alps: Pictures & Information."
http://www.wilderdom.com/evolution/OtziIcemanAlpsPictures.htm (Accessed January 6, 2008)

31 Jill A. Fisher, "Tattooing the Body, Marking Culture." Body & Society: 91-107. 2002 Sage Publications
http://bod.sagepub.com/cgi/content/abstract/8/4/91 (Accessed January 6, 2008)

32 Chuck Brank, "Lyle Tuttle, the Forefather of Modern Tattooing", Prick Magazine Feature,
http://www.prickmag.net/lyletuttleinterview.html (Accessed Jan 20, 2008)

33 "Bono Falls" YouTube http://www.youtube.com/watch?v=YjiAGPswkuY (Accessed Jan 23, 2008)

34 Edna Gundersen, "Bono Recalls Pontiff's Affection for the Poor—and Cool Sunglasses." USA Today,
4/4/2005
http://209.85.165.104/search?q=cache:qhhzOyaUG0IJ:www.usatoday.com/life/people/2005-04-
03-pope-bono_x.htm+pope,+bono,+sunglasses&hl=en&ct=clnk&cd=1&gl=us (Accessed January 25,
2008)

35 FOXNEWS.COM Report: "Angelina Jolie Splits Leather Pants at 'Beowulf' Premiere," Monday, November 12, 2007
http://www.foxnews.com/story/0,2933,310603,00.html?sPage=fnc/entertainment/jolie (Accessed
January 25, 2008)

36 Brian Sack "ebay: DKNY Leather Pants I Unfortunately Own," Banterist, 9/16/2005
http://www.banterist.com/archivefiles/000286.html (Accessed January 27, 2008)

37 "Cool Cities and Un-Cool Countries" Dialog International
http://www.dialoginternational.com/dialog_international/2007/08/cool-cities-and.html (Accessed
Jan 30, 2008)

38 Ibid.

Part 2: The Science of Cool

1 Donnell Alexander, "Are Black People Cooler Than White" Utne Reader, (Might Magazine) November/December 1997
http://www.utne.com/issues/1999_84/view/950-1.html (Accessed February 2, 2008)

2 Randy Atlas, "What is Swing" http://syrswingdance.org/swing.html (Accessed February 2, 2008)

3 "Transcript of Jeremiah Wright's Speech to NAACP" CNN Politics.com April 27, 2008
http://www.cnn.com/2008/POLITICS/04/28/wright.transcript/ (Accessed April 30, 2008)

4 "Donna Summer: Orgasmic Vocals" Anecdotage.com,
http://www.anecdotage.com/index.php?aid=19882 (Accessed February 5, 2008)

[5] Jeremy Dutton and William Puchert, "Music Industry Responds to Terrorism." *Zephyr*. October 10, 2001

[6] Craig D. Lindsey, "Whitney's Dookie Bubble" *Houston Press*, July 14, 2005 http://www.houstonpress.com/2005-07-14/music/whitney-s-dookie-bubble/ (Accessed February 8, 2008)

[7] John Lewis, "Tony Bennett" AARP, *The Magazine*, July/August 2003

[8] "Sammy Davis Quotes," braineyquote.com

[9] Pat H. Broeske, "A High Life After Death: The Candy Man Can" *New York Times*, June 3, 2007

[10] "Sammy Davis Quotes" brainyquote.com (Accessed February 2, 2008)

[11] "Whoopi Goldberg Quotes," brainyquote.com (Accessed February 5, 2008)

[12] "Whoopi Goldberg Defends Ted Danson's Blackface Act at Friars Club" Jet Encyclopedia http://www.encyclopedia.com/doc/1G1-14488564.html (Accessed February 10, 2008)

[13] Ellesse Chow, "Inspirational Stories V: Whoopi Goldberg, Survivor Personified, Goal Setting College," http://www.goal-setting-college.com/inspiration/whoopi-goldberg/ (Accessed February 6, 2008)

[14] Justin McCarthy, "Whoopi Goldberg Latest to Attack 'The View's' Elisabeth Hasselbeck on Abortion" LifeNewscom, October 5, 2007 http://www.freerepublic.com/focus/f-news/1908012/posts (Accessed February 12, 2008)

[15] Melena Ryzik, "Timberlake, Pop Juggernaut, Is Gaining Some Unusual Appeal" *New York Times* http://www.nytimes.com/2007/02/07/arts/music/07just.html?_r=1 (Accessed February 15, 2008)

[16] Ibid.

[17] Renee Hopkins Callahan, "The Neurology of Creativity" Idea Flow, March 15, 2004 http://ideaflow.corante.com/archives/2004/03/ (Accessed February 15, 2008)

[18] Stephen M. Endelson Ph.D., "Theory of Mind" Autism Research Institute http://www.autism.org/mind.htm

[19] Steve Silberman, "The Geek Syndrome" *Wired* http://www.wired.com/wired/archive/9.12/aspergers_pr.html (Accessed February 20, 2008)

[20] Ibid.

[21] Brett Sowerby, "My Chemical Romance Talks to The Campus" 9/20/07 http://media.www.mainecampus.com/media/storage/paper322/news/2007/09/20/Style/My.Chemical.Romance.Talks.To.The.campus-2979744.shtml (Accessed February 13, 2008)

[22] Jennifer Kahn, "If You Secretly Like Michael Bolton, We'll Know" *Wired* 10/04 http://209.85.165.104/search?q=cache:9KgbHafHdlMJ:www.wired.com/wired/archive/12.10/brain.html+brain+science,+cool&hl=en&ct=clnk&cd=6&gl=us (Accessed February 20, 2008)

[23] "The Learning Style of a Typical Student" The Learning Web, Chapter #3, page 130 http://www.the-learningweb.net/chapter03/page130.html (Accessed February 28, 2008)

Part 3: The Business of Cool

[1] Lisa Picarille, "The Lure of Youth" *Revenue Today*
http://www.revenuetoday.com/print.php?name=The+Lure+of+Youth (Accessed March 1, 2008)

[2] "State of the World 2004: Consumption by the Numbers" Worldwatch Institute
http://www.worldwatch.org/node/1783 (Accessed March 4, 2008)

[3] "Man Behind the Five Million Pound Dress" *Northern Echo*, July 20, 2004
http://archive.thenorthernecho.co.uk/2004/7/20/45238.html (Accessed March 8, 2008)

[4] "Fendi Sues Wal-Mart for Selling Counterfeit Bags" ShortNews.com, June 10, 2006 http://www.short-news.com/start.cfm?id=54918 (Accessed March 10, 2008)

[5] Interview, Dee Dee Gordon and Sharon Lee, PBS, Frontline, "The Merchants of Cool,"
http://www.pbs.org/wgbh/pages/frontline/shows/cool/interviews/gordonandlee.html (Accessed March 10, 2008)

[6] "Flagpole Sitting" everything2, Feb 6, 2002
http://everything2.com/e2node/flagpole%2520sitting (Accessed March 14, 2008)

[7] "Socrates, Shop Talk" Anecdotage.com
http://www.anecdotage.com/index.php?aid=4308 (Accessed March 15, 2008)

[8] Andrew Clennell, "Violent Video Game Sells Out After Being Blamed for Murder" *The London Independent*, 8/5/04
http://findarticles.com/p/articles/mi_qn4158/is_20040805/ai_n12796110 (Accessed March 16, 2008)

[9] "Alternative Marketing Vehicles: The Future of Marketing 'To One'" *ACNielsen*
http://www.acnielsen.com/pubs/2003_q2_ci_alternative.shtml (Accessed, March 18, 2008)

[10] "PR Stunt Fallout" *The Patriot Ledger* 2/1/07
http://ledger.southofboston.com/articles/2007/02/01/news/news03.txt (Accessed March 3, 2008)

[11] Michelle Kessler, "IBM Graffiti Ads Gain Notoriety" *USA Today* 2/6/02
http://www.usatoday.com/tech/news/2001-04-25-ibm-linux-graffiti.htm (Accessed March 12, 2008)

[12] Colin Moynihan, "Neighborhood Report: Lower Eastside/East Village; Mysterious Sidewalk Messages Deciphered, and Banished" *The New York Times* 10/3/99
http://query.nytimes.com/gst/fullpage.html?res=9A03E3D9133EF930A35753C1A96F958260 (Accessed March 24, 2008)

[13] "Zune Guerilla Marketer Arrested at SXSW"
http://gizmodo.com/gadgets/portable-media/zune-guerrilla-marketer-arrested-at-sxsw-244276.php (Accessed March 20, 2008)

[14] Deborah Branscum, "US: Marketing Under the Radar" in *CorpWatch*. Dec 22, 2004
http://www.corpwatch.org/article.php?id=11762 (Accessed March 23, 2008)

[15] Ibid.

[16] "First Americans Set to Drive the BMW Hydrogen 7 on US Roadways 8/16/07" Source BMW 8/17/07 www.autobloggreen.com/2007/08/17/ will-ferrell-gets-first-bmw-hydrogen-7-for-regular-use-on-us-roa/ (Accessed March 12, 2008)

[17] "Alternative Marketing Vehicles: The Future of Marketing 'To One'" *ACNeilson* http://www.acnielsen.com/pubs/2003_q2_ci_alternative.shtml (Accessed, March 18, 2008)

[18] Ibid.

[19] Ibid.

[20] "Tom's Pubic Ad Avoids Ban" Daily News, Vogue.com 2/27/2003 http://www.vogue.co.uk/vogue_daily/story/story.asp?stid=9026 (Accessed March 16, 2008)

[21] "Brits Having Fun With Dog Breath Ad" http://www.adrants.com/mt335/mt-search.cgi?IncludeBlogs=1&search=wrigley&x=0&y=0 (Accessed March 5, 2008)

[22] Carrie McLaren, "As Advertisers Race to Cover Every Available Surface, Are They Driving Us Insane?" Issue #18 of *Stayfree magazine*. http://www.stayfreemagazine.org/archives/18/adcreep.html (Accessed March 12, 2008)

[23] Joe Kovacs, "Unborn Baby Threatens Mom in New Burger Ad" *WorldNet Daily* 4/15/05 http://www.wnd.com/news/article.asp?ARTICLE_ID=43793 (Accessed March 20, 2008)

[24] Sonya Reyes, "Hebrew National Rolls Out Mom Squad" *Brandweek*, 5/28/01 http://findarticles.com/p/articles/mi_m0BDW/is_22_42/ai_75286748 (Accessed March 5, 2008)

[25] Michelle Orecklin, "There's No Escape" *Time* 4/30/03 http://www.targetedmediapartners.com/in_the_news/Time_Mag.htm (Accessed March 2, 2008)

[26] "37,375" payday: That's Using Your Head!" Associated Press 1/25/05 MSNBC http://www.msnbc.msn.com/id/6867209/ (Accessed March 3, 2008)

[27] "Karolyne Smith" BEMEZINE.COM Encyclopedia http://wiki.bmezine.com/index.php/Karolyne_Smith (Accessed March 3, 2008)

[28] Daniel Terdiman, "For Rent: Your Forehead for $5,000" CNET News.com, 8/17/05 http://www.news.com/For-rent-Your-forehead-for-5,000/2100-1024_3-5837180.html (Accessed March 3, 2008)

[29] Brenda Goodman, "A New Name for Sale? No Way for a Marine" *New York Times*, 12/13/06 (Accessed March 6, 2008)

[30] Mitch Albom, "Branded Kids: Next Step in Culture's Fall - Jason Black Selling Naming Rights for Son to Highest Bidder" *Los Angeles Business Journal*, 8/6/01 (Accessed March 3, 2008)

[31] "Fashion Trends in Contemporary Japan" *Japanese Fashion* http://www.twinisles.com/japan/culture/c002.php (Accessed March 1, 2008)

[32] PBS, Frontline, "The Merchants of Cool," http://www.pbs.org/wgbh/pages/frontline/shows/cool/tour/tour2.html (Accessed March 8, 2008)

[33] Ibid.

34 "Milli Vanilli-Blame it on the Rain" Music and Entertainment,
http://tn1294894.bluemtnblogs.com/taglink45/tag/milli+vanilli+story (Accessed March 2, 2008)

35 Colin Devenish, "Ashlee Booed at Bowl" *Rolling Stone*, 1/5/05,
http://www.rollingstone.com/artists/ashleesimpson/articles/story/6806632/ashlee_booed_at_bowl
(Accessed March 4, 20008)

36 "Eminem: I Didn't Lip-Sync" StarsWeLove.com, 11/9/04
http://www.starswelove.com/scriptsphp/news.php?newsid=4880 (Accessed March 6, 2008)

37 "Britney Spears: Gimme More MTV Video Music Awards 2007"
http://www.youtube.com/watch?v=hdhV16_u7ow (Accessed March 1, 2008)

38 "Hannah Montana Caught Using Body Double" Associated Press, 1/11/08
http://www.msnbc.msn.com/id/22612282/ (Accessed March 4, 2008)

39 "Ready to Rumble: Tyson Serious About Fighting Women on 'World Tour'" *Sports Illustrated.com*
10/16/06
http://sportsillustrated.cnn.com/2006/more/10/16/tyson.tour.ap/index.html (Accessed March 3, 2008)

40 "Simpson Opts for Extra Help Because of Acid Reflux" Associated Press 10/26/04
http://www.msnbc.msn.com/id/6322824/ (Accessed March 2, 2008)

41 Diana Pemberton-Skies, "Haute Couture: The History of Fashion" The Sideroad
http://www.sideroad.com/Clothing/haute-couture.html (Accessed March 4, 2008)

42 "Fines for Droopy Drawers Backed" BBC News, 2/9/05
http://news.bbc.co.uk/2/hi/americas/4249831.stm (Accessed March 3, 2008)

43 Donnell Alexander, "Are Black People Cooler Than White" *Utne Reader, (Might Magazine)* November/December 1997
http://www.utne.com/issues/1999_84/view/950-1.html (Accessed February 2, 2008)

44 David Kunzle, "Fashion and Fetishism" The Corset Trade in the Later 19th Century
http://www.corsets.de/The_Corset_Trade_in_the_Later_19th_.php (Accessed March 4, 2008)

45 Andrew Buncomb, "Breast Implants? Forget it. Nose job? Been there. Now it's Toe Surgery to Fit into Your Bling-Bling Shoes" *The Independent*, 12/8/03
http://www.independent.co.uk/news/world/americas/breast-implants-forget-it-nose-job-been-there-now-its-toe-surgery-to-fit-into-your-blingbling-shoes-575936.html (Accessed March 8, 2008)

46 Randall Beach, "Man Gets 14 Years in City Slaying" *New Haven Register.com*
12/15/07http://www.nhregister.com/WebApp/appmanager/JRC/BigDaily?_nfpb=true&_pageLabel=pg_article&r21.pgpath=%2FNHR%2FNews%2FNew+Haven&r21.content=%2FNHR%2FNews%2FNew+Haven%2FTopStoryList_Story_1273271 (Accessed March 12, 2008)

47 "The Safety of Silicone Breast Implants," 1999, the *National Academies Press*, page 21,
http://www.nap.edu/openbook.php?isbn=0309065321&page=21 (Accessed March 24, 2008)

48 Jilia Sommerfeld, "New Generation of Breast Implants Creates Buzz, Worry," The Seattle Times,
6/20/04

http://seattletimes.nwsource.com/html/health/2001960617_implants20m.htm (Accessed March 12, 2008)

[49] "New Boobs for Graduation: The Rise of Plastic Surgery as a Graduation Gift" *Trendhunter Magazine* 5/8/07
http://www.trendhunter.com/trends/new-boobs-for-graduation-plastic-surgery-as-a-grad-gift (Accessed March 6, 2008)

[50] "History and Description of Belladonna," *The Encyclopedia of Psychoactive Plants*
http://www.a1b2c3.com/drugs/bell001.htm (Accessed March 6, 2008)

[51] Diane Mapes, "Suffering for Beauty has Ancient Roots" MSNBC Health 1/11/08
http://www.msnbc.msn.com/id/22546056/ (Accessed March 28, 2008)

[52] Cardinal Pallavicini (Italian Cardinal and Historian, 1607-1667) *Vita di Allessandro VII*

[53] "Pete Burns Sues for £1m Over Botched Lip Implant Surgery" *Daily Mail* 1/25/07 http://www.daily-mail.co.uk/pages/live/articles/showbiz/showbiznews (Accessed March 28, 2008)

[54] PBS Frontline, "The Merchants of Cool,"
http://www.pbs.org/wgbh/pages/frontline/shows/cool/tour/tour3.html (Accessed March 8, 2008)

[55] The Uncoolhunter.com
http://www.theuncoolhunter.com/home.php?idioma=ENG&id_categoria=13 (Accessed March 6, 2008)

[56] Courtenay Smith and Sean Topham, *Xtreme Fashion,* Prestel Publishing LTD. London. Pages 24-27

[57] "First Nude Flight Leaves Miami Bound for Cancun" NBC5.com 5/5/03
http://www.nbc5.com/travelgetaways/2179262/detail.html (Accessed March 4, 2008)

[58] The Uncoolhunter.com
http://www.theuncoolhunter.com/home.php?idioma=ENG&id_categoria=13 (Accessed March 6, 2008)

[59] Ibid.

[60] Ibid.

[61] Katherine Knight, "The Crying Game: Misery Clubs Come to the UK" *The Daily Mail* 4/9/07
http://www.dailymail.co.uk/pages/live/femail/article.html?in_article_id=447434&in_page_id=1879 (Accessed March 5, 2008)

[62] Charles Young, "Rock Is Sick and Living in London" 1977, *Rolling Stone.* (Accessed March 6, 2008)

[63] Mark Cooper, "The Sex Pistols: Winterland, San Francisco, *Record Mirror*, Jan 28, 1978

[64] Sex Pistols Website, http://www.thefilthandthefury.co.uk/ (Accessed March 15, 2008)

[65] Ibid.

[66] Owen Gibson, "Rotten Outburst Sends ITV into Tizzy" *Guardian.co.uk*,
http://www.guardian.co.uk/media/2004/feb/04/realitytv.broadcasting (Accessed March 29, 2008)

[67] Karl Quinn, "Everyone's a Winner" theage.com.au
http://www.theage.com.au/news/Music/Everyones-a-winner/2004/11/19/1100748195505.html
(Accessed March 5, 2008)

Part 4: The Coolhunter's Field Guide

[1] Pico Iyer, "The Unknown Rebel" *Time Magazine*, The Time 100, Leaders and Revolutionaries, April 13, 1998
http://www.time.com/time/time100/leaders/profile/rebel.html (Accessed April 5, 2008)

[2] "Susan B. Anthony" http://www.history.rochester.edu/class/suffrage/Anthony.html (Accessed April 8, 2008)

[3] "Disputation of Doctor Martin Luther on the Power and Efficacy of Indulgences" by Doctor Martin Luther 1517
http://history-world.org/martin%20luther.htm (Accessed April 16, 2008)

[4] "Rockefeller Controversy" Diego Rivera Collection
http://www.diego-rivera.org/rockefellercontroversy.html (Accessed April 3, 2008)

[5] Andrew Boyd, *Daily Afflictions* W.W. Norton, New York 1/02

[6] "Alexander Calder" (1898-1976)
http://www.ubu.com/film/calder.html (Accessed April 5, 2008)

[7] Salvador Dali: Biography Buzzle.com http://www.buzzle.com/articles/salvador-dali-biography.html
(Accessed April 5, 2008)

[8] Richard Pearson, "Andy Warhol, Pioneer of Pop, Dies at 58, After Heart Attack" *Washingtonpost.com* 2/23/87
http://www.washingtonpost.com/wp-srv/style/longterm/review96/fishotandywarhol.htm (Accessed April 6, 2008)

[9] Stephen Silverman, "Grammy Winner Ray Charles Dies at 73" *People,* 5/10/04
http://www.people.com/people/article/0,,649778,00.html (Accessed April 18, 2008)

[10] Donnell Alexander, "Are Black People Cooler Than White People?" *Utne Reader (Might Magazine)*
http://www.utne.com/1997-11-01/are-black-people-cooler-than-white-people.aspx (Accessed April 18, 2008)

[11] Earwig Music, Artist Bios, "Louisiana Red"
http://www.earwigmusic.com/NewSite/ArtistBios.asp (Accessed April 23, 2008)

[12] Today's Woman Writing Community: "Biography of Langston Hughes"
http://www.todays-woman.net/article1666.html (Accessed April 13, 2008)

[13] "Woodie Guthrie, Biography" http://xroads.virginia.edu/~1930s/RADIO/woody/bib.html (Accessed April 16, 2008)

[14] "Friedrich Nietzsche," BrainyQuote, http://www.brainyquote.com/quotes/authors/f/friedrich_niet-zsche.html (Accessed April 15, 2008)

[15] Anne Applebaum, *washingtonpost.com* 2/2/06 http://www.washingtonpost.com/wp-dyn/content/article/2006/02/01/AR2006020101837.html (Accessed April 11, 2008)

[16] Theo Richmond, "Victim of His Imagination, The" *The Spectator*, 4/27/2002 http://findarticles.com/p/articles/mi_qa3724/is_200204/ai_n9067984/pg_2 (Accessed April 25, 2008)

[17] "Author Margaret P. Jones Admits She Faked Gang Memoir" *The Huffington Post*, 5/6/2008

[18] Josh Aterovis, "Heavy Metal Becoming More Gay-Friendly" http://www.afterelton.com/music/2005/8/metal.html?page=0%2C1 (Accessed April 28, 2008)

[19] Ibid.

[20] Jack Tapper, "Sinead Was Right" 10/12/02 *Salon* http://dir.salon.com/story/ent/feature/2002/10/12/sinead/ (Accessed April 10, 2008)

[21] Guerrilla Girls Website, http://www.guerrillagirls.com/ (Accessed April 7, 2008)

[22] Grace Jones Biography, Net Glimse, http://www.netglimse.com/celebs/pages/grace_jones/index.shtml (Accessed April 12, 2008)

[23] "Rock 'n' Rule" *Telegraph*.co.uk 8/1/06 http://www.telegraph.co.uk/arts/main.jhtml?xml=/arts/2006/01/08/svblair08.xml&page=3 (Accessed April 29, 2008)

[24] "Cool's Hot and Cold Constituency: Obama Inspires a Story on Style" Democratic Underground, 2/24/08 http://www.democraticunderground.com/discuss/duboard.php?az=view_all&address=108x126164 (Accessed April 27, 2008)

[25] Caryn James, "Television/Radio; Bachelor No 1 And the Birth of Reality TV" 1/26/03 *The New York Times* http://query.nytimes.com/gst/fullpage.html?res=9400E0D61330F935A15752C0A9659C8B63&sec=&spon=&pagewanted=all (Accessed April 23, 2008)

[26] Ibid.

[27] "The Idol Star Who Can't Sing," CNN.com 2/23/04 http://www.cnn.com/2004/SHOWBIZ/Music/02/23/music.idoldreamer.ap/index.html (Accessed April 5, 2008)

Conclusion

[1] Socrates, "Vain Protest" Anecdotage.com http://www.anecdotage.com/index.php?aid=366 (Accessed May, 1, 2008)

Photo Credits

p. 11 (bottom): Library of Congress, Prints and Photographs Division p. 16: ©iStockphoto.com/DaddyBit p. 11 (top): Library of Congress, Prints and Photographs Division p. 20 (bottom): ©Prisma/SuperStock p. 23 (left): ©iStockphoto.com/blaneyphoto p. 23 (right): ©iStockphoto.com/Rodrigo Blanco p. 24 (top): ©iStockphoto.com/Limber p. 24 (bottom): ©iStockphoto.com/Limber p. 26 (top): ©Patrick Hertzog/AFP/Getty Images p. 26 (bottom): ©iStockphoto.com/Frank Wright p. 28: Library of Congress, Prints and Photographs Division, Carl Van Vechten Collection p. 29: ©iStockphoto.com/Jon Schulte p. 37: ©CBS Photo Archive/Hulton Archive/Getty Images p. 38: ©iStockphoto.com/Henry Chaplin p. 41 (top): ©David Fenton/Hulton Archive/Getty Images p. 41 (bottom): ©Central Press/Hulton Archive/Getty Images p. 46: ©Chris Walter/WireImage/Getty Images p. 49 (top): ©Sebastian Pfuetze/zefa/Corbis p. 49 (bottom): ©James Devaney/WireImage p. 51: ©iStockphoto.com/Joe Augustine p. 55 (top): ©iStockphoto.com/Brandy Taylor p. 55 (bottom): ©iStockphoto.com/Sharon Dominick p. 57: ©iStockphoto.com/Dave White p. 63 (top): ©iStockphoto.com/Matthew Scherf p. 63 (bottom): ©iStockphoto.com/4x6 p. 65: ©iStockphoto.com/creacart p. 66: ©iStockphoto.com/Justin Horrocks p. 67: ©iStockphoto.com/David Meharey p. 86: ©Columbia TriStar Television/courtesy Everett Collection p. 92 (left): ©Paramount/courtesy Everett Collection p. 92 (right): ©Fotos International/Hulton Archive/Getty Images p. 93: (left): ©Michael Rougier//Time Life Pictures/Getty Images p. 93 (right): ©CBS/courtesy Everett Collection p. 95 (left): ©Paramount/courtesy Everett Collection p. 95 (right): ©Paramount/courtesy Everett Collection p. 97: ©Terry O'Neill/Premium Archive/Getty Images p. 100 (geek): ©iStockphoto.com/Ryan Lane p. 100 (emo): ©iStockphoto.com/Joe Augustine p. 100 (brain): ©iStockphoto.com/Master_Hajan p. 109 (top): ©Lindsay Brice/Michael Ochs Archives/Getty Images p. 109 (bottom): ©iStockphoto.com/Eliza Snow p. 112 (kitten): ©iStockphoto.com/Michael Chen p. 112 (gnome): ©iStockphoto.com/John de la Bastide p. 113 (geode): ©iStockphoto.com/Nick Stone p. 114 (left): ©John Shearer/WireImage/Getty Images p. 115: ©iStockphoto.com/Kenneth C. Zirkel p. 118 (left): ©iStockphoto.com/Evgeny Kan p. 118 (right): ©iStockphoto.com/Henk Bentlage p. 119 (left): ©iStockphoto.com/Jim Pruitt p. 119 (right): ©Belinda Wright/National Geographic/Getty Images p. 121 (left): ©iStockphoto.com/David Falk p. 121 (right): ©iStockphoto.com/shearman p. 127 (bottom): ©Scott Gries/ImageDirect/Getty Images p. 131 (top): ©AP Images p. 131 (bottom): ©Tony Duffy/Getty Images p. 142 (top): ©iStockphoto.com/Diane

About the Author

Marianne Taylor was the winner of *Ms. Magazine*'s 2005 Fiction Contest. Her short stories have appeared in *The Boston Review, Dogwood, Fresh Yarn, The Ledge, The Briar Cliff Review* and others. Recently, she co-authored the black humor classic, *The Starving Artist's Survival Guide*, a must-have book for struggling creative types.

Marianne teaches Visual Art and Media Literacy in the public schools of Brookline, MA. Her involvement with the Media Literacy movement (which teaches students how to de-construct the onslaught on modern advertising and other media) has generated much of Ms. Taylor's interest in the evolution of fads as well as the packaging and selling of all things cool.